Life Plans

Life Plans

&

LOOKING FORWARD TO RETIREMENT

Grace W. Weinstein

Holt, Rinehart and Winston
New York

To my parents:
Esther and Dave
Helen and Hy

———————

Published by Holt, Rinehart and Winston,
383 Madison Avenue, New York, New York 10017.
Published simultaneously in Canada by Holt, Rinehart and Winston of
Canada, Limited.

Library of Congress Cataloging in Publication Data
Weinstein, Grace W.
Life plans.

Includes bibliographical references.
1. Retirement. I. Title.
HQ1062.W43   301.43'5   78-12310
ISBN Hardbound: 0-03-039691-3
ISBN Paperback: 0-03-039696-4

First Edition

Designer: Karolina Harris
Printed in the United States of America
1 3 5 ⁻ 9 10 8 6 4 2

Contents

1245

Foreword

Retirement is a fact of life. With or without mandatory retirement there comes a time, in most people's lives, to put aside the day-in, day-out responsibilities of employment and move on to other things. Many people look ahead to this new stage of life and prepare for it. But too many people view preparation through a narrow lens, planning only for the financial changes retirement inevitably brings. Few people use a wide-angle lens; few people view retirement in terms of its overall personal impact. Most books, with their emphasis on the financial, perpetuate this one-sided view.

This book is designed to fill the gap, to help you plan your retirement to meet your individual needs and interests—and to identify those individual needs and interests. It deals with the use of time, with where to live, with personal relationships, and with money, all in the context of self-understanding. It deals with you, and with your retirement: a new and potentially exciting stage of life.

Acknowledgments

This book could not have been written without the research of countless gerontologists, psychologists, and sociologists. It most certainly could not have been written without the shared experiences of men and women who are retired or in the midst of preparing for retirement, among them many readers of my column in *The Elks Magazine.*

I would like particularly to express appreciation to Robert C. Atchley, Director, the Scripps Foundation; James M. Mulanaphy of Teachers Insurance and Annuity Association-College Retirement Equities Fund; Sidney B. Simon of the University of Massachusetts; Phoebe Bailey, Eastern Regional Coordinator of Action for Independent Maturity, the pre-retirement planning arm of the American Association of Retired Persons; Walter S. Wikstrom of The Conference Board; and Gordon F. Streib of the University of Florida at Gainesville. Their insight was incalculable. I thank them.

Thanks, too, to Claire M. Smith for her continued support and available ear. And, never last, my appreciation to Esther Horowitz for typing to perfection.

Myths and Facts

1
Retirement Is . . .

True or False? Retirement:
- is a major source of stress.
- has always signified the final stage of life.
- is more often enjoyable when voluntary, unhappy when forced.
- affects all men, but few women.
- leads most people to pull up roots, frequently to move south in search of the sun.
- is synonymous with aging; both bring declining health and a sense of uselessness.
- varies little, once it begins.

The correct response to every one of the above statements is *False*. Yet many people, informed intelligent people, have fallen prey to one or more of these myths. Many people, as a result, look ahead to retirement with unwarranted dread. This dread is not only misplaced, it exacts a tremendous toll—because *the way in which you look ahead makes a great deal of difference.* Research clearly shows that your attitude, as you approach retirement, is enormously important. Those who look ahead to a positive experience in retirement, according to a long-range study by

Cornell University, are likely to find it so; those who anticipate the worst may find it waiting for them.

What's your attitude, right now, toward retirement? Are you:

- looking forward to taking life easy?
- worried about loss of income?
- not sure what you'll do with your time?
- thinking glumly about hanging around the house all day?
- making a list of places to visit?
- anxious to spend more time on your woodworking?
- pretty sure you'll get used to the whole idea?
- looking into community needs you can fill?
- depressed at being thought of as old?

If your thoughts are somewhat negative, now is the time, once and for all, to dispel the myths.

RETIREMENT IS NOT A SOURCE OF STRESS

A list of stress-producing events has been popularized in recent years, a list that includes death of a spouse at the very top and runs through many other life changes. Retirement itself is fairly high on the list, and other changes that frequently accompany retirement— change of financial status and of residence, changes in personal habits and in social activities and in recreational pursuits—produce stress of their own.

Yet retirement, according to countless retirees, is not a source of stress at all. It is the *anticipation* of retirement that is more universally stressful; the actuality works out just fine. "Fantasies tend to be negative," says Yale University psychologist Daniel J. Levinson, "and life turns out to be better." Anxiety peaks before retirement, over such real uncertainties as the adequacy of income and loss of occupation or relationships with on-the-job friends. But income usually turns out to be adequate, other activities replace the job, and new friends take their place beside old ones.

Both individual experiences and sociological studies indicate that the vast majority of men and women, doom-and-gloom reports notwithstanding, like retirement and get used to it very quickly. Generally good feelings about life, a positive sense of well-being, come through time and time again. "What I wish someone had told me about retirement is that it could be so much *fun,"* a teacher wrote to *Retirement Living* magazine. "I liked my work and I hated to leave. I wondered what I would do with myself in retirement. . . . But then I found myself adapting much more easily than I'd expected to a new way of life. I began to enjoy my freedom, my spirits rose, my horizons were expanded. . . ."

RETIREMENT IS A NEW SOCIAL PHENOMENON

The whole concept of retirement is relatively new. It has become widespread, universally accepted, and universally expected only in the last couple of decades. Some people have always retired, of course, because of ill health or to pursue other interests, but most have worked until the end of life. Most expected to do so. As recently as 1950, 46% of the men in this country over the age of 65 were still in the labor force. By 1970, so rapidly has the concept spread, only 25% of men over 65 were still working.

The whole issue of forced retirement, of employer-determined and -enforced retirement age, is even newer, a product of social and economic factors unique to our times: slowed economic growth, an emphasis on youth, jobs that require an all-or-nothing approach, and perhaps above all, an increasing life-span.

When jobs are plentiful, experience is valued. Older workers, with their accumulated wisdom and maturity, are in demand. When jobs are scarce, as they are in periods of restricted economic growth and high unemployment, there is only one way to make room for the young: by retiring the old. "New blood" is the rallying cry; "room at the top" is the motivation. And older workers who would like to continue (others, of course, are eager to retire) are shoved aside.

An emphasis on youth in the culture as a whole only adds fuel to the fire. Discrimination against older people—what Dr. Robert Butler, director of the National Institute on Aging, has called "ageism"—grows out of a culture that worships youth. In fashion, in behavior, in appearance, youth is dominant. Mandatory retirement, once again, makes way for the young. Mandatory retirement, now under attack as a matter of "fairness," may disappear as a matter of pragmatism. As the birthrate continues to decline and the postwar population peak moves on in years, society may need more workers than the under-65 population can supply.

Forced retirement, meanwhile, is also related to the all-or-nothing jobs produced by increasing urbanization. In rural societies there is always something for older people to do; they may slow down but they are rarely forced to stop. The shepherd can watch his flock, the farmer tend a smaller plot. Some lucky souls in our urban culture still have the option of tapering off—the executive who can become a part-time consultant, the salesman who can reduce his route, the self-employed professional who can cut back on office hours—but most employees do not. When employers demand unflagging energy and full-time commitment, they often, justifiably or not, turn to younger workers. Although many older workers are just as energetic as, and more dedicated than, younger workers, the easy way out mandates fixed-age retirement for all.

The lengthening life-span has also had major impact. When life expectancy was 48.2 years, as it was for a man born in 1900, there was no need for mandatory retirement policies. A man born in 1974, in contrast, can expect to live an average of 68 years; a woman born the same year can look forward to nearly 76 years. The man who is currently sixty-five, more to the point, can expect to live thirteen more years, while his wife, at the same age, can look forward to eighteen years of life. Employers, no doubt picturing employees in their seventies and eighties doddering around the office (just the way Supreme Court justices dodder around their chambers), have fixed retirement policies at or about sixty-five. Such policies are fairly recent; they may, given increasing public debate, be temporary.

MANDATORY AND VOLUNTARY RETIREMENT ARE SIMILAR IN MANY WAYS

Although the debate centers around the issue of forced retirement, most employees expect to retire. Most employees want to retire, want to turn their attention to new pursuits after forty or so years on the job. Many are retiring early, just as soon as pension plan or employer permit. Yet even when retirement is voluntarily elected, even when it is elected early, retirement may hold some surprises. The employee who is forced to retire may expect to be unhappy, expect to miss the job; retirement may prove instead, especially with planning, to be delightful. The employee who chooses to retire, on the other hand, is frequently faced with an unanticipated sense of loss; retirement may turn out to be emptiness instead of leisure, boredom instead of relaxation.

Most of us simply don't realize just how much the job supplies. Even where we think all it meant was a paycheck, there is what Dr. William F. Westlin, director of medical services at Sandoz Pharmaceuticals, characterizes as an "emotional support system, the structure and routine and identity and friends and associates and responsibilities and satisfactions that go with the job—including knowing where you will be and what you will be doing for eight hours a day, five days a week." Part of this support system is position and authority; every job, except perhaps the very bottom line, offers some sense of authority. Part of it is personal identity. How often do you characterize yourself as what you do? I'm a teacher, a doctor, an engineer, a mechanic?

And another part of the support system, a part it would seem easy to relinquish, involves constraints, limitations on your time and energies, restrictions on your freedom to go as you please and do as you please. Yet the loss of constraints, Dr. Westlin suggests, still constitutes loss, a loss of the structure that forms your days. No one expects you to be anywhere at a certain time, you can sleep as late as you like—and instead of relief you feel a sense of loss. "There are fewer plop, plop, fizz, fizz days," says a former university athletic director. "Not as many daily deadlines, fewer meetings, no great necessity to hurry, hurry, hurry—but how do you stop? You get up at the same time, go like crazy for a couple of hours, and by 9:30 A.M. everything is done. The days are longer. . . . People don't need you the way they did before. And that's tough to get used to."

The only way to get used to it, whether you plan to retire or are asked to retire, is to plan the replacement of your support system in advance. You must plan what you will do with your time, to lend structure to your days and meaning to your life. That's what this book is all about.

WOMEN AND MEN ARE BOTH AFFECTED BY RETIREMENT

Most retirement literature is directed to men. But all women, whether or not they have worked outside the home for extended periods of time, must also look ahead to retirement. Women are affected by retirement in every possible way: as working singles, as nonworking wives who must cope with their husbands' retirement, as working wives who must mesh their own retirement with that of their husbands', as "displaced homemakers" forced into the labor market by widowhood or divorce and later forced to retire, as late-in-life voluntary re-entrants to the labor force who cherish the independence (both financial and emotional) of the job and relish the social contacts as well.

More and more women are working outside the home for more and more years. In 1900, when a woman's life expectancy was 50.7 years, her work-life expectancy was 6.3 years. In 1974, when her life expectancy was 75.0 years, her work life averaged 23.0 years. More women work throughout their lives and still more women leave the work force but return to it. Right now, a majority of 45- to 54-year-old women are in the labor force, facing the same retirement situation as men. Many of these women, married or not, have career commitments as strong as those of men. Sometimes, because of the odds women have faced in making careers and the determination necessary to face those odds and win, the commitment is even stronger.

Women, therefore, face exactly the same retirement issues as men. Women have exactly as much need to plan for retirement. It is wrong to assume, as some gerontologists have assumed, that retirement is not a problem for working women because "they always have a job to do at home." Some women are glad to return to that job. Others bitterly resent the assumption. "I juggled managing an office and managing a home for thirty-five years. Now I'm supposed to just stay home. Cleaning the house—I'm very well-organized after all these years—takes maybe an hour; I certainly haven't any interest in making it take longer." This executive bookkeeper is angry at forced retirement, just as angry as a man might be. She would also be better off, just as a man would be, if she had taken the chance to know herself and to plan her retirement in advance.

TO RETIRE IS NOT NECESSARILY TO MOVE

Many people believe that giving up one's home goes along with giving up one's job. Along with the gold watch at the retirement dinner goes the predictable question: "Where are you going to live?" The actual answer for most people: "Right here, where I've always lived."

Most retirees do not move. Of those who do, few move very far. Just 2% get as far as crossing a state line; only 5% of that 2% moves to an age-segregated community. Most older adults, too, maintain independent households, alone or with a spouse; only 12% live with their children and 4% in institutions. Those who *are* institutionalized, furthermore, are far older than they used to be.

The average age of nursing home residents is now seventy-eight. Most older people maintain independent households in the communities where they have lived for years.

RETIREMENT IS NOT SYNONYMOUS WITH AGING

Retirement, although it usually occurs relatively late in the life-span, has nothing to do with aging. Most people retire at sixty-five. Health does not begin to decline, on the average, until the mid- to late-seventies. Most retirees are among the group University of Chicago sociologist Bernice L. Neugarten calls the "young-old," active and energetic and able to make the most of their lives. Many pre-retirees, unfortunately, do not realize this, do not think far enough ahead. "If I'd expected to live this long," says one bored but healthy eighty-one-year-old, "I would have figured on doing something besides playing golf."

Some people think that health declines because of retirement. Not so. If anything, health may improve, once the stresses and strains of the daily grind are removed. Enforced idleness may lead to chronic illness, as the American Medical Association points out, both physical and mental. Yet retirement need not be and should not be synonymous with idleness. Those who want to be idle may be idle; no one else is required to sign up for idleness just because of retirement.

Gerontologists, furthermore, assert that, if you discount those who retire *because* of ill health, the health of retirees is as good as, sometimes better than, the health of others the same age. Only one out of five of those over sixty-five is restricted by ill health; only one out of twenty is institutionalized. And there are one million people in this country over the age of ninety, 14,000 over the age of one hundred. There is some inevitable slowing down with age, although there are enormous individual differences, but most older people are healthy enough to actively enjoy life.

Age itself is always relative. There are young eighty-year-olds and old forty-year-olds. There are people who are fit and trim and healthy into their seventies and beyond and there are people who run to flab and let their muscles deteriorate at thirty. If anything, individual differences may become more pronounced with age; there is more evident similarity among a group of twelve-year-olds than among any group of sixty- or seventy-year-olds. Chronological age is just a convenience of the calendar, nothing more.

We do, eventually, age. But aging itself does not automatically mean ill health. Robert Butler points out, in his landmark book *Why Survive?,* that "the exciting aspect of medical care for the elderly is that much of what has long been considered to be aging is disease. Many of the ailments of the old are possibly preventable, probably retardable, and most certainly treatable." Actual senility is rare; many instances of diagnosed senility are actually manifestations of untreated disease. Health problems that do crop up, therefore, should not be passed off as an inevitable part of the aging process, something you just have to live with. Diseases treatable at forty-five are treatable, by and large, at seventy-five, and treatment should be sought. It helps, of course, to go into retirement in the best possible health; proper diet and exercise still go a long way toward forestalling ill health.

If you subscribe to the myth that retirement and aging are two sides of the same coin, then you may also subscribe to the myth that mental rigidity, inability to learn, and feelings of uselessness are part of retirement. None of these myths is true. Intellectual ability does not diminish with age; the old can learn as well as the young, if sometimes a bit more slowly. Psychological flexibility also remains intact. It resembles physical aging in this respect: there are people who are young in heart all their lives and there are people who solidify and lose their capacity for growth at twenty-five.

You probably have more capacity for learning than you recognize. Look at it this way: If you're in your sixties, close to retirement age, you have lived through enormous change, change to which you have had to adapt in order to survive. That ability to adapt does not come to an abrupt halt at any particular birthday; it may even improve with age.

Physical changes in your lifetime have been enormous, in transportation and communication and living conditions. Social change has been even more enormous, more of a test of psychological flexibility. One eighty-nine-year-old woman, pioneer of the one-piece bathing suit, remembers being arrested for removing her stockings before a swim; now bathing costumes have given way to bikinis. Marriage used to be traditional when people cared about each other; now people—perhaps your own children or even a widowed parent—live together without marriage. Marriage used to be forever; today one out of three marriages ends in divorce. You may frown at some of these changes, but you have adapted. Your adaptation is evidence of the never-ending human ability to learn and to change, of your own capacity for growth.

Many people believe that being older inevitably means not feeling needed, being lonely, not having enough money, fear of crime. These are real problems, to be sure, faced by significant minorities of older people. But the word is minority. Most older people, the vast majority, do not face these problems—although even they think others do. One of the most significant findings of a nationwide survey conducted by Louis Harris Associates in 1974 for the National Council on the Aging (NCOA) is that people under 65 and people over 65 share the same misconceptions about what it is like to be over 65.

For example, 54% of the public at large felt that "not feeling needed" is a serious problem faced by those over 65; only 7% of respondents over 65 found this to be a personal problem. Loneliness was expected to be a problem by 60% of the general public and by 56% of those over 65; it was reported as a serious problem in actuality, by just 12% of those over 65. Not having enough money, similarly, was expected to be a very serious problem by 62% of the public and 59% of the older public; financial worries actually affected 15% of those over 65. Thirty-seven percent of the general public and 33% of those over 65 thought that most retirees would have a hard time finding enough to do to keep busy; only 6% of retirees found time heavy on their hands. You get the idea. People who are active, busy, and comfortable in retirement tend to see themselves as exceptions. They are not.

A similar discrepancy crops up in the NCOA report with respect to personality factors. Only 25% of those over 65 think that people over 65 are friendly and warm; 72%, however, characterize themselves in these terms. A close 33% and 34%, respectively, characterize others over 65 as bright and alert and as open-minded and adaptable; 68% and 63% refer to themselves this way. Only 38% think their peers are good at getting things done; 55% of those over 65 know that they themselves are good at getting things done. Once again, fact collides with fiction. The majority of older people are warm and outgoing, bright and alert, open-minded and adaptable, and good at getting things done; brainwashed by a youth-oriented society, they think of themselves as exceptions when they are not. Put all this in personal terms: if you are capable and in control of your life at forty-five or at fifty-five you should still be so at sixty-five and, barring ill health, at seventy-five as well. There is no automatic shutoff.

THE RETIREMENT EXPERIENCE IS AN INDIVIDUAL EXPERIENCE

Although retirement is, for most people, a rewarding time of life, it is a new experience. The initial adjustment to this new experience may take some time. It may go through several phases. At the end, your retirement will be what you make of it.

The retirement event—luncheon, dinner, just saying good-bye on the last day of work—is an unmistakable turning point. It is often coupled with exhilaration. But the exhilaration is, for some people, followed by letdown. Most people settle into a comfortable retirement pattern right away; some go through a series of stages, in which shifting moods are normal. Robert C. Atchley, director of the Scripps Foundation and a noted researcher in the field of retirement, has identified several psychological stages. If you know about them, it may help.

The first is a "honeymoon" phase in which the newfound freedom is exciting. This is the busy time, the time for catching up on all the household repairs, trying new hobbies and expanding old ones, traveling, seeing grandchildren, and so on. "The person in the honeymoon period of retirement," says Dr. Atchley, "is often like a child in a room full of new toys. He flits from this to that, trying to experience everything at once."

Disenchantment, unhappily, sometimes comes next, especially for people who thrive on routine and who have not established a satisfying routine in retirement. People who take the time to develop outside-of-work interests while they are still working are less likely to suffer from disenchantment.

Disenchantment may be a temporary problem for those who don't need routine but think they should. "I was afraid I'd be bored, and I said yes to every organization in town; I was miserable until I extricated myself because I had no free time at all." People who truly enjoy the absence of routine will do just fine, once they understand themselves. Retirement planning, it can't be emphasized too much, is an individual matter. Some people must have routine, a structure to their days; others don't want it, don't need it, and do perfectly well without it. The first may think ample time for golf is all he wants from retirement—and be climbing the walls after three weeks. The second really is content, to golf or not, and let the days slip by.

If disenchantment does set in, it is usually followed by reorientation. This is a second try, a new and usually successful stab at finding a personally satisfying way of life. Most people find contentment right after the honeymoon; almost all of the rest find it after disenchantment and reorientation.

Whether you find contentment, and when, depends to a very large extent on your attitude and on the kind of planning you do long before retirement. There's little point in being negative. Retirement can be unpleasant if you insist on mourning the past instead of building the future. It can be a time of bitter resentment if you allow yourself to feel rejected by society, shunted aside by an active world. It's far more productive to be positive. At least, look at retirement as a time to let go, to relax, to be yourself. At best, as it should be, make your retirement a positive stage of life, an opportunity for growth and renewal.

Plan ahead for retirement. Take responsibility for your own life. Decide what you want to do and go ahead and do it. But first, to make your life work for you, know yourself.

Know Yourself

2
Who Are You?

Who are you? "What do you mean, who am I? That's obvious. I'm Bob Jones. I'm sales manager for the Widget Corporation." Yes, but who are you? "Well, I'm a married man, with one youngster grown, one still in college. I live in Smithtown. I'm active in the Lions Club." Yes, but who are you? What do you like and dislike? What—and who—is important to you? What makes you angry? What makes you proud? What do you value?

Most of us wrestle with these questions of self-identity, if at all, as emotion-torn teen-agers. Some question again at a midpoint in life. But most, once settled into a path, once wrapped up in job and family and community, seldom stop to ask, "Who am I? Where am I going? Why?" We seldom have time to ask, even if we want to. Now, as you look ahead to retirement, take the time. Pause, take a deep breath, and look at yourself. Look at where you are, and look at where you're heading.

Retirement offers a fresh start. It's a time when, for the first time in a long time, all the options are yours. No parent, no teacher, no army sergeant, no employer, is going to tell you what to do and when to do it. You have total freedom. But total freedom, as delightful as it sounds after years of being in harness, can be mind boggling. We all need some direction. And the absolutely best direction to set the retirement course is self-knowledge. Find out who you really are. Decide what you want out of retirement. Then, and only then, start to make your plans.

A SELF-PORTRAIT

The process of self-examination may be fun. It should, at least, be enlightening. Start by asking yourself some questions. For example: Am I someone who:

- is anxious to get things done?
- likes to be alone?
- is usually right?
- finds children annoyingly noisy?
- thinks most people are honest?
- welcomes gifts?
- will try new foods?
- tolerates disagreement?
- gets bored easily?
- thinks being on time is important?
- reads a lot?
- watches baseball on TV?
- puts money away for a rainy day?
- trades in a car every year?
- exercises regularly?
- prefers my family to other people?
- worries about what I don't get done?
- easily loses my temper?
- maintains childhood hobbies?
- works well as part of a team?
- likes to travel?
- has many close friends?

These questions, based on values-clarification techniques developed by Sidney B. Simon of the University of Massachusetts, won't give you a full self-portrait. But, if answered honestly, they may begin to provide an awareness of self beyond "Bob Jones who lives in Smithtown." They may show you a fairly narrow way of life, restricted by habit, as one man found; he determined to open up, to try new things before retirement narrowed his world still further. Or they may indicate a person already open to experience, welcoming change and receptive to the new horizons of retirement. Whatever your personal discoveries, you may, if you like, expand self-awareness by going a step further: give the questions (these, and as many as you would like to add) to a spouse or close friend; ask that person to guess how you answered the questions about yourself. See if your answers agree. If they don't, there is a gap between the way you see yourself and the way others see you, a gulf between your thoughts and your actions. Which image do you prefer? Which will you want to act upon?

Here's another clue in the treasure hunt of self-understanding. Empty your wallet. What do you find? There is documentation, of course, the proof that you exist, have a home, can drive a car. But what else is there? Pictures of family and friends? Scraps of paper with old telephone numbers? Tickets for a concert or a football game? Old keys to unknown locks? Receipts for gifts long since given? Other people's business cards? The collection tells a story about you. The man with a complete set of family photos, dog-eared from frequent display, is people oriented. The woman with a collection of business cards and appointment reminders is clearly absorbed in her career. And the person with nothing at all but documentation, with a wallet devoid of trivia, is neat and methodical and maybe, just maybe, devoid of consuming interests.

Here's another eye-opener, in the form of incomplete sentences. Complete each one as quickly as possible.

• If I were the boss . . .

• When things aren't going my way . . .

- I'm proud that I . . .
- I'm looking forward to . . .
- I wish my wife/husband . . .
- I like working with people who . . .
- My friends don't know I think . . .
- My children . . .
- My biggest mistake was . . .
- I know I can . . .
- When I retire . . .

There are no "right" or "wrong" answers to exercises of this sort. But honest answers do lead to self-understanding. And self-understanding is necessary, if retirement is to fulfill its promise, because each person is an individual, with individual needs and likes, values and attitudes. Satisfaction is found in different ways, in as many different ways after retirement as before. There are guidelines for successful retirement, therefore, but no rigid rules. Each retirement must be individually planned. Self-understanding and self-acceptance come first.

Without self-understanding we find the man who has dreamed for years of retiring to a fisherman's paradise, who buys a cottage by the lake, who retires there, and who finds, after three weeks or maybe five or six, that he can't fool himself any longer: he is both lonely and bored out of his mind. Without self-understanding we find the couple who retires to the Southwest, after looking forward to the climate and recreational opportunities, only to find that the family and friends left behind make even the northern winters look appealing. Without self-understanding, too, we find the woman so worried about inactivity that she schedules her retirement days full to the brim with community service activities, only to discover that she has substituted new pressures for old ones; what she really wants is an unscheduled life, free from responsibilities and the strictures of a clock.

One reason for such mistakes is sheer lack of planning, a head-in-the-sand approach that puts off decisions until the last moment and then, under the pressure of immediacy, makes some wrong ones. One reason is the wrong kind of planning, planning based on generalization, planning based on some mythical "ideal." There is no ideal retirement. Pulling up roots and moving to a warm climate is refreshing for some retirees and total disaster for others; embarking on a second career is the right course for some, a blind alley for others. One reason is a lack of self-understanding, of knowing what one *really* enjoys doing and why. And one reason is that self-understanding gained at one stage of life may be inappropriate at another stage. In many ways we remain the same; the girl of twenty is always within the woman of sixty. Yet, in other ways, we do not remain the same at all. We grow and change with experience. Your wallet may contain a residue from previous interests and activities; a diary kept long ago may reveal another "self." How could I have done such things? you ask. How could I have been so silly? *Now* I understand my parents. On another front, a life of unrestricted leisure may please a young adult but be frustrating to the same person after years of productivity. The goal put off for years for lack of time may no longer challenge when time is at last at hand.

How can we, then, avoid such mistakes in planning our own retirement years? We have to separate, first, the way we live from what we are; we must divorce the roles we play from our basic selves. Don't bother with detailed self-psychoanalysis, but do try to understand yourself well enough to know what kind of retirement planning is appropriate. If you love to fish on vacation because you are by nature a philosopher, enjoying your own thoughts more than the company of others, you may thrive in a retirement built around fishing. If you love to fish on vacation because it provides a total change from an otherwise frantic way of life, you may soon become bored when fishing is all there is. Does challenge and stimulation turn you on or unnerve you? Do you prefer a placid, well-ordered life?

To find out, look beyond the superficial, beyond easily applied labels. It's easy to label Jon an extrovert, a glad-hander, a joiner because, although brusque at times, he is generally outgoing and friendly, a welcome addition to every club, organization, and gathering. It's tempting to call Evan an introvert, quiet and self-sufficient, because he is generally pleasant and calm; he seldom takes the lead in a group but does contribute useful ideas. George may be labeled compulsive, driven to get ahead, constantly working, constantly striving. Mary is easygoing; nothing seems to bother her. In actual fact, of course, the extrovert may be fighting innate shyness. Introvert Evan and easygoing Mary may be as compulsive as George beneath the surface calm. And George himself, who would really rather take life easier, is pushing himself to prove that he can succeed.

PERSONALITY AND THE ROLES WE PLAY

If these thumbnail sketches prove anything, therefore, it is that surface behavior does not necessarily reflect personality. Personality is the inner self, shaped by a combination of innate abilities and lifelong experience. Personality certainly affects behavior. But outer influences also affect behavior, and personality, the real "self," can be disguised by the roles we play. We all, unknowing actors, play many roles. We play roles we choose and those which are chosen for us. We play social roles to suit ourselves and to suit others. The "uniform" of the jeans-clad teen-ager or the pinstripe-suited banker is an outer reflection of role-determined behavior, of behavior which reflects the expectations of others. We play some roles temporarily and some permanently; we act as students when we are students but we act as males or as females throughout life. We play quite a few roles at once, playing the child to our parents and the parent to our children, and we play other roles which succeed one another.

Bob Jones, at the beginning of this chapter, defined some of his roles in his answer to the question Who are you? He defined himself as worker, husband, father, community resident, and

1245

organization participant. He is also, of course, a man. Being a man in our society is a specific role with specifically defined behavior (although social change can alter the ground rules, making traditionalists uncomfortable). He is also a gardener, a golfer, a son, a brother, an uncle, a neighbor. And he is middle-aged, a fact which also determines behavior.

Age roles shape behavior in part because other people expect them to do so, in part because we ourselves share the expectation. We insist that people "act their age," says sociologist Bernice L. Neugarten, and then proceed to tell them what acting their age means. It means, she says, that there is "a time in the life span when men and women are expected to marry, a time to raise children, a time to retire." Young people are breaking this age stratification to some extent. They are getting married when they want to, or not at all. They are refusing to follow the traditional dictates of age norms. Adults may find it harder to break loose. But you owe it to yourself not to be locked in by someone else's idea of age-appropriate behavior. Act yourself. As anthropologist Ashley Montagu, a vigorous seventy-two, points out, "when an older person simply behaves like a normal healthy human being, he seems younger."

Culturally ascribed sex roles also influence behavior. Men have traditionally been expected to be providers, women to be nur-turers; men have been raised to be assertive and strong and dominant, women to be passive and weak and dependent. Men and women tend to view themselves in terms of these expectations. Men, in one study, rate themselves as ambitious, assertive, calm, competitive, guileful, hostile, reasonable, and self-controlled. Women in this study (especially younger women) rate themselves more highly as charming, cooperative, easily embarrassed, easily hurt, friendly, helpless, sincere, sympathetic, and timid. There have always been exceptions, of course. There have always been sensitive men and independent women. And these rigid expecta-tions in any case, like those of age roles, are beginning to break down. But the changes, again, may have more impact on the younger generation. Those of us nearing the retirement years were socialized in an earlier era, influenced by an earlier set of expectations.

Changes in long-standing roles of any kind, roles in which we've become comfortable, inevitably have an impact—even if the change is anticipated and welcome. For men, for example, life's major role has been work. Retirement is sometimes viewed as traumatic because it ends that major role. For women, life's major role has traditionally been as wife and mother. Retirement from that role, when children leave an empty nest behind, has long been seen as traumatic. Yet many men find their self-esteem in roles outside of work. Almost half the men in one California study, interestingly, lived lives centered on wives, children, and grandchildren. Retirement, far from being traumatic, is a welcome experience for these men. Many women, more and more, are filling significant roles outside the home, finding self-esteem in work. These women may be bothered more by retirement than by the empty nest. And many stay-at-home women, far from being upset at the empty nest, revel in the newfound freedom, in the opportunity to make a new life for themselves and their husbands. "It's a second honeymoon," one notes. "It's just us."

For some there is no trauma at all in retirement. For others, the trauma lies in unexpected areas. "The only problems I anticipated were financial problems," says one rueful retiree. "They turned out not to exist. I had planned well, and expenses went down along with income. But emotional problems were something else. My wife and I hadn't spent so much time together in years; we started bickering all the time."

This kind of trauma can be anticipated, and forestalled, if we recognize that retirement, welcome or not, has an unmistakable impact on the roles we play. It ends some roles, most notably that of worker. In doing so, it increases the time available to play other roles, as community participant, family member, and hobbyist. It changes the quality of some roles. More time together, for instance, affects any couple accustomed to just evenings and weekends of togetherness. And perhaps most important, it allows us to choose the roles we prefer, to substitute self-selected and personally meaningful activities for the routine of work. It allows us, at last, the opportunity to select activities really suited to individual likes and dislikes, suited to personality.

LEISURE TIME

Clues to personality, to the things we really value, can be found in what we do with leisure hours during our working years. Freely selected leisure activities, not the golf game designed to woo clients or the club joined to make contacts, are the important clue. Look at your present leisure activities. To what extent are they related to your work? To what extent can you—and do you—make time for preferred activities? Surprising amounts of our "leisure" time are directly related to work. The salesman who spends "free" hours entertaining clients, the teacher who must prepare for the next day's class, and the person too exhausted by work to do anything but fall asleep in front of the television set—all have their leisure constrained by their work. All, in fact, are missing out on leisure and on the rejuvenating benefits of leisure.

Look again at your present leisure activities. To what extent are they things you do alone? with others? To what extent are you involved with your family? outside the home? The family-centered individual spends leisure hours at home, the community-centered person is a joiner, active in clubs and organizations, seeking organized entertainment. The family-centered might turn his carpentry skills to building a backyard climber for his grandchildren; the community-centered might raise funds for a community playground. "I love to travel," says the family-centered. "There's nothing like getting in the car and going down to visit the grandchildren." "I love to travel," says the community-centered. "I like to go on organized tours; it's exciting to visit different countries."

What do you choose to do in your free time? How much really

free time do you have? Do you have a hobby? more than one? When was the last time you devoted any time to your hobbies? Do your "favorite" activities include woodworking equipment gathering dust, a collection of coins long forgotten on the shelf? Ask yourself:

- Does the time drag when you're not at work? Or do you find that there aren't enough hours to do everything you would like to do?
- Do you like to get out and around when you have time off? Or is your favorite leisure sport a spurt of relaxation around the house?
- Do you spend leisure hours with friends? relatives? the immediate family? Or do you enjoy being alone?
- What do you want from your leisure activities? physical exercise? a sense of accomplishment? recognition?
- Do you like to try new activities? or stick to the tried-and-true?

Ask yourself what you get out of your present leisure pursuits. Identifying the pursuit is not enough. The same activity can provide different rewards at different times and for different people. Simply watching television, to take an all-too-common example, can be leisure of many sorts. It may be pure entertainment for one individual, a way to wind down after the day's work for another. It may be a social science assignment for a student, a competitive necessity for a network executive. It isn't television itself, and it isn't always the individual viewer, that decides the use to which it is put.

Even when leisure appears to be leisure, in short, there is sometimes a subtle or not-so-subtle relationship with work. Three types of leisure have been identified: unconditional, complementary, and coordinated. Of the three, only the first is not related to work in any way. *Unconditional* or for-its-own-sake leisure is the only type which is both freely chosen and undertaken for its own sake. As such, it is the only type of leisure which provides any clue to personality. If you take an evening course in bridge because you think it would be fun, this is unconditional leisure. Whether the fun stems from the intellectual challenge of the game or from the opportunity to make congenial friends, is is still unconditional leisure. If you take the same course because your co-workers and clients all play bridge and you want to be able to socialize with them, it becomes *complementary* leisure instead—not required by your job but expected of you because of the work you do. Complementary leisure, which is not quite freely chosen, describes the corporate executive who heads the United Fund Drive and the steelmaker who belongs to the union, as well as the manager who learns to play bridge—or golf. Any one of these people might really prefer to do something, anything, else; they don't feel they have the choice. *Coordinated* leisure, the third type, is freely chosen but it is still indirectly related to work. It is characterized not by the salesman who must entertain clients but by the engineer who chooses to read a professional journal to keep abreast of developments in the field.

Work influences leisure, clearly, in many ways. It constrains our leisure by limiting our time and, sometimes, our energy. It also determines, to a greater or lesser extent, the kinds of leisure we choose. And it affects the quality of the leisure. Leisure during our working years provides a counterpoint to work: the deskbound office worker may deliberately choose physical exercise; the outdoorsman may prefer more sedentary recreation. Because of the direct relationship between work and leisure, some, but not all, leisure activities carry over well into retirement. The hobbies and activities selected only because they provide welcome relief from the mental tension or physical exertion of work may no longer be meaningful. Some new activities may have to be selected to take their place.

In any event, the leisure pattern of your working years will influence your retirement years. If you feel good about community service for its own sake, you will continue to be active after retirement. If you enjoy puttering around the house, the garden, and the workshop, you will continue to do so after retirement. But if all or most of your leisure activities are work related, if you are quickly bored with any leisure and anxious to get back to work, watch out. Retirement may be deadly, both figuratively and literally, unless you develop some other interests. The time to do so is now.

You can take the reins, get control of your life. But lifelong habits do continue to influence the retirement years, to the extent we allow them to do so. Lifelong habits of leisure have an impact: "I've always been bored when I'm not working." So do lifelong habits of dealing with problems, coping with crisis: "I can't help it, I'm a worrier."

COPING WITH STRESS

Retirement may or may not be stress producing, but it is a new stage of life. As such, it requires some adjustment. The way in which you've adjusted to situations throughout life, the way in which you've coped with change and with stress, will be the way, by and large, in which you cope with adjustment to retirement. People who can anticipate crises, rather than allowing themselves to be taken by surprise, do better. Worrying, like daydreaming, can be positive if it leads to workable solutions. So do those who view crises as challenges rather than threats. A challenge is something you can rise to meet; a threat is intimidating.

How do you cope with stress? What's your style? Before you answer, you might try keeping a journal for a couple of weeks. Record any situation, big or not-so-big, which produces stress or tension. The major ones are obvious: the death of a close friend, the loss of a job, sickness. Others, not quite so major but nonetheless tension producing, occur regularly: an argument with your spouse, a bad day on the job, a carpentry project that failed, a rained-out golf game, a drop in the stock market, a disagreement with your children—or your parents.

After keeping tabs for a while, review your journal. How many situations did you regard as stressful? How many were a challenge? or a threat? How did you respond to stressful situations? When you disagreed with your spouse, or with your boss, did you:

* walk away without saying anything?
* calmly explain your point of view?
* try to talk but lose your temper and wind up yelling?
* feel misunderstood and unappreciated?
* call on others for support?
* settle the disagreement at the time?
* eventually forget about it?
* stay angry for several days?
* make up on the surface but continue to feel hurt?

When weather spoiled your golf game, did you:

* stay home and sulk?
* do something else? go to a museum or a movie, play cards, or read a book?

When your job wasn't going well, did you:

* start to think about changing jobs?
* consider a brand-new career?
* hang in there and wait till things improved?
* discuss the situation with your employer?
* discuss your concerns with your spouse?
* keep your thoughts to yourself until you reached a decision?

We all handle stress differently. Some people thrive on stress and need not avoid it. They are, says Hans Selye, pioneer researcher into stress, life's "racehorses," spurred onward by pressure. These are the people energized by deadlines, motivated by competition. Others, life's "turtles," do better without stress, in a nonpressured, placid environment. These are the people who develop ulcers under tension.

We all perceive stress differently, too, perhaps depending on whether we are racehorses or turtles. One man's stress is another man's shrug of the shoulders. "I don't know what I'll do after I retire," says the first, "and I'm worried sick about whether I'll have enough money." "What, me worry?" says the second. "Things have always worked out in the past." One man moves on through life without a quiver while another tenses up at every transition, seeing a crisis around every corner. Some people withdraw, burrow into themselves, when confronted with a stress-producing situation; some seek support from others. Some people become defensive; others spring to the attack. Some anticipate stress; others are disturbed only by the unexpected. Some people resist change and cling to the status quo; others, more flexible, view change as an opportunity for growth.

How you cope with stressful situations is significant. How you feel about the way you cope is significant, too. Are you satisfied? Or would you be happier if you didn't withdraw or fly off the handle or whatever? We do follow long-standing habits of response, just because they are habits, but habits can be broken. The first step, in a procedure used by psychologist Frances Meritt Stern in her stress-reduction courses for businessmen, is to categorize the things you find stressful. Divide them into things that can be changed and things that cannot be changed. Divide them into things related to yourself, to others, and to situations.

Then try to change what can be changed, and desensitize yourself to what cannot be changed. "Retirement is retirement is retirement," says Dr. Stern. The issue won't go away. But your response to it can change. Think about a specific issue you find stressful: mandatory retirement, for example. How do you view it? Is it something personal? directed against you? Is it a fact of nature? Is it an arbitrary decision by a particular company? Is it the final insult life has to offer? Is it a chance to move on to a new stage of life? Some people view retirement as situational, as an objective fact; others view it as something others are doing to them. Which view you hold determines how you cope. It also determines how angry and stressful and anxious the whole experience will be. If you can view retirement objectively and recognize it as unchangeable, you can desensitize yourself to its impact by deliberately thinking of something pleasant when you think of retirement, such as a trip you will finally have time to take. Then, instead of being fixed in a futile battle against retirement, you can move on to decide what you're going to do with the rest of your life. Failure to do so makes the pre-retiree like the teen-ager who looks ahead to being married, Dr. Stern points out, but who never looks beyond the chapel. There is life after marriage—and there is life after retirement.

Change isn't necessarily easy. It takes conscious effort, constant awareness of what we are actually doing and what we wish to be doing, but it can be managed. And it's definitely worthwhile. Flexibility, including the ability to go beyond stress and to adapt to new situations in new ways, is one of the most useful tools in meeting any of life's challenges, including the challenge of retirement.

RETIREMENT PATTERNS

Successful retirement, of course, like successful life, need not follow a single pattern. People age successfully, adjust to retirement successfully, in many different ways. Some, according to one major study, welcome retirement as a time free from job-related pressures, a time to devote to personal enthusiasms and activities both old and new. "I can hardly wait until I can take early retirement" says a printing-shop manager. "I carve figures in wood, and I want to devote more time to my carving." Others may also welcome retirement, but because they need do nothing at all; it's a time in which "I don't plan to do one damn thing." And some don't like the idea of retirement, resist it as long as possible, but adjust well as long as they keep busy; they often work part-time or set up a fixed schedule of volunteer activities. In every case, among the eighty-seven men in the study, "personality characteristics changed very little throughout their lives. Those who felt a need to keep busy had always tried to keep busy; those who blamed others for their frustrations and failures had always done so. . . ." The way we live at thirty and at forty, it seems, has a great deal to do with the way we live at sixty and at seventy. Those dissatisfied in later life, according to a significant forty-year study of another group of men and women, were those who were dissatisfied in earlier years. Those who are open to new experiences in young adulthood continue to be so later on.

But don't throw up your hands in resignation. Personality is never static. Growth continues to the end of life. Developmental psychologists used to devote all their energies to children, thinking that "grown-ups" were all finished growing. Recent research, however, conclusively demonstrates what personal experience has long made many of us suspect: we do not stop growing on any magic birthday. Adults continue to grow and change, to go through transitional periods and stable periods, just as children and adolescents do. Personality traits may remain the same, but personality as a whole can change. If one trait remains the same while another changes, says Daniel J. Levinson, the Yale University psychologist who has made significant contributions to contemporary understanding of adult development, the entire pattern is altered. If you've become more self-confident as you've matured, with experience gained on the job, that confidence will affect all your relationships. If you've weathered a midlife crisis, whether or not you've made major changes in your life, that experience itself has made you grow. Personality is shaped, and reshaped, by experience.

In some respects, too, men and women grow more alike as they age. Men tend to become more people oriented, more sensitive to feelings and emotions, more involved with family.

Women, once freed of familial responsibilities, often become more assertive and independent. Older women, in fact, often tend to be dominant, a factor which can influence the marital relationship in significant ways. The sensitive older man, however, still bears within him the ambitious young man and the career-oriented middle-ager. The dominant grandmother carries within her, always, the shy young bride and the dependent woman of her early adulthood. We remain the same, in many ways, yet we are different, as we adapt to change and as we change ourselves.

One of the important changes takes place in late adulthood, at about the time of retirement, as we redefine ourselves in relation to work, to our families, to society at large, and to ourselves. This redefinition, while significant, need not be stressful or traumatic. We've come to expect high-growth periods of life, such as adolescence, to be conflict ridden, yet some teen-agers go through these years with a minimum of turbulence. Some young people, to be sure, are tossed about, seemingly out of control; many others stay in command; others fluctuate wildly. The time of mature adulthood that corresponds with retirement may be compared to adolescence in many respects, Dr. Levinson points out. This, too, can be a conflict-ridden period, a time of turbulence but also of change and growth. This too, is a normal part of the life cycle.

This particular transition, in any event, is a perfect opportunity for personal growth. Use the freedom to grow. Keep an open mind, try to respond flexibly to new situations, to be curious and open and enthusiastic, and psychological growth will continue to the very end of life. So will personal satisfaction.

Who you are, and what you can become, is not related to your age. Age is chronological; it measures the passage of calendar time. Age is biological; it measures the growth and decline of the body and its separate parts. Age is functional; it measures capacity. And age is psychological; it measures what you think you can do and what you think you can't. "Aging is a matter of mind over matter," it has been said. "If you don't mind, it doesn't matter."

People who don't mind are too busy living; people who "think young" act young. People who remain psychologically flexible, tolerant of change, adjust well to retirement. If you've been flexible all along, you're one step ahead. If you've had trouble adjusting to change in the past, you can learn to do so in the future. It's up to you. Once you know who you are, and who you want to be, you can chart your retirement course.

3

What Do You Want to Do?

What is your ideal retirement? Surely you've daydreamed over the years, when work temporarily palled or a birthday made thoughts of retirement come to life. What is your daydream? Does it revolve around lazing in the sun? taking up ceramics? helping the retarded? or the Red Cross? traveling far and wide? giving up, at last, a job you've never liked for one you've always wanted?

How does this daydream compare to actuality, now that you're thinking seriously about retirement? How does it match your knowledge of your self? Do you really want to do whatever it is you've been dreaming about? And, if you do, will it be possible? Fantasy serves a useful purpose in pre-retirement planning, according to Robert C. Atchley of the Scripps Foundation, insofar as it serves as a "dry run," a practice session which can "smooth the transition into retirement by identifying issues requiring advanced decision-making." Fantasy can also get in the way of realistic planning, insofar as daydreams are purely wishful thinking, divorced from reality.

But don't dismiss your daydreams. Instead, for successful retirement planning, turn them to good use. Use the technique of "imagery," of structured daydreaming, to rehearse for retirement. Psychologist Frances Stern suggests: Close your eyes, take a deep breath and hold it for several seconds, then relax. Now, picture a day in your life ten years from now. Picture the day in detail:

- Where are you? What are you doing? What's happening around you? What are you feeling about what's happening?
- What kind of picture is this? Is it a drama? a tragedy? a comedy? a soap opera? a mystery?
- What is the audience doing? Are the people in your life applauding? laughing? booing? falling asleep?
- Are you comfortable with the picture? with the audience response?

The scene itself, and reactions to it, will vary with the individual. Two friends, making plans for retirement together, did this exercise. Both looked ahead ten years to similar days, days in which an early morning golf game is followed by a nap, then lunch, then gin rummy, then cocktails, dinner, and more gin rummy—all with friends of similar age. "We see each other every day," one man commented, after thinking about the picture, "and we talk about the same things—our health, the weather, and our golf game. I can't stand another day of this. My audience is falling asleep of boredom—and so am I." His friend, envisioning a similar scenario, reacted differently: "The sun always shines, my golf game gets better and better—and so does my gin rummy. I'm very comfortable with the prospect."

Look at your own daydream. If this is the scenario you want to play out in retirement, you can start to take the necessary steps to get where you want to go. If it is not, you can start to rewrite the script. You're the writer, the director, and the actor, all in one.

Before you start, however, try another exercise. Chart your life as if it were a graph. Draw a horizontal line from the beginning to the anticipated end, marking the peaks and valleys of your life experience (so far) above and below the line. Then look at the substantial length of horizontal line remaining from now until the end. Where are you now in your life? What have you accomplished? What have you failed to accomplish? What must you do to ensure, at the end, memories of a life well spent? Use these questions and answers, this "lifeline," to determine your priorities.

One fifty-eight-year-old, treasurer of a family-run business (not, however, his family), recognized that he wanted, more than anything, to leave his mark on the world, to be remembered. He saw that it wouldn't happen at business—he was not in line for the presidency—so determined to make it happen in the community. Instead of continuing to plead "no time" and "the pressure of business," he joined a regional group working to establish a hospital burn-treatment center. His organizational skills proved very effective. His community is well on its way to having the first specialized burn-treatment center in the region; and he is well on his way to assuring remembrance. If he hadn't stopped to think, however, to assess his priorities, he would not have turned his talents to this purpose. "I would have continued single-mindedly to try to forge ahead at work," he says, "even though there was really no place to go. I would have been on a treadmill to nowhere."

GOALS AND OBJECTIVES

As you determine your current priorities, then, examine the goals which rule your middle years. Look at the goals in terms of your priorities for the rest of your life. Personal goals, Dr. Atchley points out, come from three major sources: "goals we are taught and are expected to hold as personal goals; personal goals which are held by others we seek to emulate; and personal goals which grow out of our own experiences and knowledge about ourselves and our capabilities." Now, at retirement, self-determined personal goals can take the lead. You've had years of experience. You're becoming reacquainted with your "self." Use goals based on this knowledge to guide your retirement plans.

Draw up your retirement plans in terms of goals, objectives, and actions. Goals are broadly based, while objectives are specific and action sets the course. It takes well-designed action to reach specific objectives and objectives, in turn, to reach goals. Your goals should be personally meaningful; they should also be realistic.

Moving to an island in the South Pacific—or to a retirement community in the sun belt—is not a realistic goal for someone with ongoing responsibility, emotional as well as financial, for an invalid relative in Oregon. Realistic retirement goals may include such broadly based intentions as "having good friends" and "freedom from financial worries." Just stating either goal, however, will not bring you very close to achieving it. Specific objectives and detailed plans of action are needed.

In the area of friendship, specific objectives might include making new friends, of different ages, to share different activities. The detailed action plans to do so might include joining a special-interest club or making an extra effort to get to know neighbors. There are always different ways to reach the same goal. Part of successful personal planning is choosing among the alternatives. Part of choosing is seeing the consequences of each choice: What's the best thing that can happen if you choose a particular course? What's the worst? Can you live with it? One woman's campaign for friendship involved joining a community bowling league. She realized that she might feel inadequate until her bowling improved with practice, but decided that the goal was worth the possible embarrassment.

In the financial sphere, objectives might include an adequate cash reserve, income-producing investments, and ventures for profit. Detailed plans to reach these objectives might include setting aside certain amounts from each paycheck while still working, cutting back on expenditures, getting good financial advice. One couple's plan was to cut back on living expenses gradually in the five years before retirement to rehearse, painlessly, living on a reduced retirement income. Your personal hierarchy of goals, objectives, and action plans, from the general to the specific, can be charted, along with the possible consequences. Working them out on paper, in fact, may help you to focus your thoughts and get you started on the road to implementation.

It helps to understand your current goals, even though the goals of your retirement years may differ somewhat from the goals of your working years. During the working years, attention is inevitably divided between work and family. The balance differs from person to person, but success on the job is a primary goal for many. One man will actually turn down advancement on the job because it means giving up time with the family; another, more typical, will put off time with family in the interests of business. One busy industrial-equipment salesman continually put off activities with his children and his wife until "just one more" sale was made, one more deal completed. He thought, although he didn't say, that he was showing love for his family by providing for them. But he woke up one day, not surprisingly, to find his children grown and gone, his wife no longer particularly interested, and himself on the verge of retirement. Sad. Sadder still was the fact that if this man had recognized his goals and admitted them, to himself as well as to his family, acceptance (if not delight) might have been possible.

It is quite possible, of course, that your working-year goals are not even really your own. You may have adopted goals which help you to play an expected role but which do not really fulfill your personal needs or satisfy your personal sense of accomplishment. Our salesman friend could justify his absorption in work with the explanation that he was doing it all for his family. He, as it happened, really did find great satisfaction in making that sale or closing that deal. The hard-driving executive may find similar satisfactions at work. But another, equally deskbound and ulcer prone, may appear ambitious and work oriented but actually be fulfilling what he perceives as the expectations of others ("I had to go into the family business . . ." or "My wife likes the status of being an executive's wife . . ."). Given the choice, a choice available after retirement, this man may be far happier in a less demanding family-oriented life style. Retirement may provide such opportunity for you as well, opportunity to be, at last, yourself.

In order to be yourself, to make retirement the fulfilling time of life it ought to be, apply the self-understanding you have gained.

First, decide where you are. Take an inventory at the outset, suggests a former history professor, and know what you are building on. Look at the interests and skills you possess, while deciding which ones to develop for the future. Ask yourself: Am I basically active or passive? Do I take charge of a situation or follow others? Do I like nature, or do I prefer the indoor life? Do I find travel exciting and interesting or a nuisance and a bore? Do I like to work by myself or prefer to be with others? Am I capable with tools or awkward indeed? Do artistic, literary, or musical fields hold any interest? Am I reasonably good at figures, or do I shy away from balancing a checkbook? Develop as full a self-portrait as you can. Then tie in what you do, and do well, with what you like to do. They are not necessarily the same.

We don't always even know, after years of conforming to expectation, what we really prefer to do. To find out, try this exercise: On a piece of paper, list twenty things you like to do. Make them things you really like to do, big or small. A quiet chat with a close friend counts as much as a smashing victory at tennis— or at business, as long as it's something you really like to do. Think hard. Try to come up with twenty items. Now, go back over your list. Put a dollar sign next to any item that requires an expenditure of money every time you do it. You needn't count an initial expenditure. A bicycle costs money but, once owned, bike riding is free. Then, place an *A* next to any activity you really prefer to do alone, and a *P* next to any you prefer to do in the company of other people. Listening to music may be pleasant alone, more fun with others—or the other way round. Put an *R* next to any item which involves some element of risk, physical or financial or emotional. Free-fall parachuting involves obvious physical risk— but talking openly about feelings involves as much emotional risk for some people. Place the number 10 next to any item which would not have been on your list ten years ago, and a number 5 next to any which may not be on your list five years from now. Now, the clincher: put next to each item the approximate date on which you did it last.

It's possible to learn some interesting things from this simple exercise, devised by Sidney B. Simon of the University of Massachusetts. It's possible to learn, with great chagrin, that there aren't twenty things you really like to do: "work and sleep and an occasional good movie—that's all I could come up with." It's also possible, in fact downright probable, to find that it's been a long time since you've done most of your "favorite" things: "I was dismayed to see how long it's been since I walked along the ocean, or had a quiet talk with my brother." It's possible to find, if you compare lists with a spouse or close friend, that you share many interests—and don't share others at all: "I like to go to parties, and I just found out my wife goes only to please me." And it's possible to find that your closest friend could not guess what interests you most: "I guess I've never said, and I surely don't find time to do it lately, but what I really like is to work with my hands, to build things."

If the things you have listed are things you don't actually do very often, and if they are things which are not evident to those closest to you, then they may not really be things you value. Things that you value, in Dr. Simon's definition, must be carefully and freely chosen, prized and cherished. They must also be publicly affirmed and acted upon. Values, in other words, should not be a secret; they should be evident in behavior. Sometimes, of course, our values get a little lost in the press of daily life. This exercise (you can do it in your head, but it will help to write it down) can help to clarify values, get you back on the right track. If you see, for example, that you really want more time with a spouse or to walk by the sea or to work with your hands, it may be possible to make the time. It should certainly be possible after retirement—and the knowledge can help you to formulate your retirement plans.

MATCHING TODAY AND TOMORROW

Before you plan your retirement days in detail, however, look at how you presently spend your days. Estimate the hours out of every twenty-four which you spend in various activities: at work, at work-related activities, in home-related chores, in sleeping and in eating, and in recreation of various kinds, alone and with others. Would you, if you could, change the amounts of time spent on various activities? You can, you know, to a surprising extent. Look at two insurance clerks, sitting at adjoining desks in the same large open office. One takes twice as long as the other to do the same routine task, because she can never put her hands on the necessary document. One arrives home from work and, no matter how tired, jogs a mile and a half before dinner, because "it rejuvenates me, and I can enjoy the evening." The other, equally weary after the commute home from work, flops down in front of the television set to watch the evening news, then complains because there is no time or energy to see friends. Management of time, so that it serves you and not the other way round, is essential.

But given the choice, would you change your daily routine? Which activity would you give the most time? Why? What makes this particular activity special to you? Is it the activity itself? or the people you share it with? or the place in which it is performed? If work is your favorite activity, if you wish you had more time in the day to devote to work, you may have a problem with retirement—unless you develop another way to find the rewards you find in work. And you can, if you put your mind to it, and look at what those rewards are. If work is pleasant but not the focal point of your life, if other activities are at least as important, you have a head start.

But what are your rewards? Think about the week just past: Was it a good week? Could it have been better? In what way? What was the high point of the week? Did the point relate to the past, such as a successful resolution of a conflict, a long-standing disagreement with a neighbor? Did it relate to the present, an accomplishment here and now, such as winning a well-matched tennis set? Did it relate to the future, to plans made for fulfillment later, such as securing hard-to-get tickets to the season play-offs of your favorite sport? Did your personal high point have anything to do with other people? Was it an emotional high? a physical thrill? an intellectual accomplishment? Was it job-related?

Take a close look at the work you do to earn a living, and the role it plays in your life. Every occupation can be described in terms of its relationship to things, to symbols, and to people. The assembly-line worker spends his day working on things; the statistician focuses on symbols; the administrator deals with people. Each occupational group, however, also stretches along a line from supervised to supervisor. Supervisors, whether they give orders to others or work alone, without direction, are in control; the supervised, who must take orders, have less control. The factory worker can take orders on the assembly line, give them as a foreman; he is still working with things as much as with people. The administrator may be lower-echelon or upper; he is still dealing with people as much as with data.

Feelings of control or lack of control, inherent in the job, tend to carry over into off-the-job lives. They can make the difference between actively working toward a successful retirement (or any other life goal) and sitting back waiting for things to happen. There is a difference in personal style. People who like being in control are "innovators," says sociologist Zena Smith Blau; they will look for new interests, seek new friends, participate in the community. One spunky seventy-two-year-old woman I know is certainly an innovator; her friends seem to multiply by geometric progression. As two old friends retire and move south, she makes four new—and close—friends in her home town. "Conformists" also adjust to retirement, but do so by adapting to circumstances rather than changing them; "I can't make new friends at my age; I'll stick to the people I have left." Conformists, less likely to seek new friends or replace old interests with new ones, find the world narrowing as they grow older. But again, don't allow yourself to be locked in by habitual personal style. Conformists, enthusiastic about post-retirement opportunities, can become innovators; if you want to adopt new interests or make new friends, you can do so. Innovators, after a lifetime of being in control, of reaching out to experience, may elect to sit back and relax.

JOB-RELATED REWARDS

How you feel about what you do, the role your job plays in your life, is actually more important than the kind of job itself. Does your job fulfill your need for control? Or must you fulfill that need in your personal relationships? As an extreme instance, the stuff of Sunday comics, the Milquetoast of the office becomes the tyrant of the home front. Does your job satisfy your need for recognition? Or must you satisfy that need elsewhere? The dutiful cog in the corporate wheel sometimes attains more recognition as volunteer coach of the town junior soccer league. Every job fills time, but do you work (in addition, of course, to needing income) because your job is the way you would choose to occupy your time? Every job provides a place to be and, in some sense, status. Do you see your job as a source of self-respect? as a way to earn recognition from others? as a way to identify your place in the community? the only way? Every job also provides, in some measure, emotional satisfaction. Do you find in your job a purpose for your life? a sense of creativity? a way to be useful? And every job, or almost every job, provides a degree of companionship. Are most of your friends made on the job? Would you rather go to the office than spend a day at home?

Some job-derived satisfactions may be more important to you, others to your neighbor. Some may be more significant to you, others to your spouse. Although both men and women find status and authority, social relationships and recognition on the job, there may be some sex-related differences. Men, the National Institute of Mental Health has found, are more likely to value work (and leisure too) as an interesting experience in and of itself; self-expression and social relationships are not quite as important. When asked to describe their work and their feelings about retirement, they are apt to talk about the kind of work they do, the responsibilities held, and the sense of status derived from the work. "I was in charge, you see, and it was a big department." Women, on the other hand, seem very often to value work (and leisure as well) in terms of social relationships; security and self-expression are second-ranking values. "I worked with some good people, but we're going to keep in touch." This difference, I suspect, may be related to the kinds of jobs held. Women in high-ranking managerial or professional positions are as likely to miss the status and power conferred by work. Men in semiskilled or bottom-of-the-ladder positions may be as likely to miss their co-workers and the paycheck as to miss the work itself. The difference may also be related to motivation (and motivations, of course, are often mixed). The woman who takes a part-time job just to get out of the house may value social contact more than the woman who works in order to use her mind. The man who works only because he must support his family will enjoy the work experience itself less than the man who sought specific training so that he could fill a particular job.

We all, men and women, invest varying portions of our "selves" in the work we do. At one extreme is the person for whom work is only a necessary evil, a means to support the real life outside the job. For this person retirement may be an economic problem but never an emotional one. People who work hard but not for the sake of work itself usually have no trouble adjusting to retirement. Their goals can be satisfied through new activities. At the other extreme is the "workaholic," the individual who lives only for work. This person, totally identified with the role of worker, is least likely to plan for retirement and most likely to find it a crisis. The workaholic, whether the stereotypical corporate figure, driven by ambition, or the blue-collar worker with no outside interests ("I played poker for four days, and couldn't wait to get back to work"), can adjust to retirement. New goals, however, must consciously be substituted for old ones. Workaholics have more often, in the past, been male, just because of cultural expectations. Women may paint themselves into the same unhappy corner, however, according to sociologist Gordon Streib, if paid employment is allowed to appear the best possible means to personal satisfaction.

Two other personality "types" are the people-oriented and the loner. Men and women who are people oriented, who center their lives around relationships with others, often find retirement very pleasant—especially if their jobs have not been people centered. If they have dealt with people on the job, as in teaching or social service, new relationships in retirement can afford equal satisfaction. One social worker, for instance, long accustomed to working with groups, found great pleasure after retirement in volunteer counseling on a one-to-one basis. Loners, on the other hand, people who prefer not to be involved with other people, may view retirement as either a threat or a relief. It's a threat if it thrusts them into closer relationships, a relief if it removes them from human contact at work. Adjustment to retirement, for these men and women, depends on the ability to remain detached. One such man was pleased as punch with his post-retirement job as night elevator operator: "I almost never have to waste my time with small talk."

Examine your work-life goals. Then think about whether your goals need be redirected in retirement. You may be lucky enough to have personal goals which can hold fast through retirement. The group case worker, above, continued to meet goals, previously fulfilled on the job, through volunteer work after retirement. A people-oriented chemical engineer who feels really useful when acting as a weekend Big Brother to young men who need an adult male in their lives, thereby meeting personal goals through after-hours activities, is thinking about becoming a resident "parent" in a group home after retirement.

You may recognize that a change of direction will be necessary after retirement. Maybe you're a social worker who has had enough of people after forty years; maybe you're a chemical engineer who has had enough of being useful. And you may not be sure of what your personal goals actually are. If you've submerged them over the years in the quest for job security and advancement, as many people have, now is the time to rediscover who you are and apply that knowledge to setting new goals for the retirement years.

Fewer than 15% of us, fortunately, male or female, are totally devoted to work, totally devoid of other satisfactions. Most of us enjoy our work, but have plenty of other interests as well; those other interests can easily be expanded to provide both meaning and pleasure in retirement. For example, my neighbor, a cosmetics salesman, enjoys being out and meeting people in his travels from store to store—but spends every spare moment either creating jewelry of his own design or refinishing furniture picked up in weekend flea-market expeditions. His only complaint is insufficient time.

MOTIVATIONS

For most of us, for whom work is more than just a source of income, there are complex motivations behind our selection of the work we do. The cosmetics salesman is gregarious. He really enjoys the daily chitchat with customers. Recognizing this, he sees that he may want to get out of his basement workshop at least part-time after he retires. He is thinking about selling some of his jewelry, on consignment, to local boutiques—a venture which would, again, take him from store to store, but at times of his own choosing.

Some of us aren't so lucky. Maybe you fell into a job years ago that was never quite right but never quite wrong enough to give up. Maybe you needed the money at the time, or the security. Given the choice—or the opportunity conferred by retirement—you might prefer to do something else. Picking the right "something else," now or after retirement, can be a lot easier if you understand the motivations involved. Ask yourself the following questions. Is it important to me:

- to be recognized in the community?
- to work with a well-known company or institution?
- to see the results of my efforts?
- to learn from what I do?
- to do something useful?
- to use my leadership abilities?
- to have a title?
- to help others?
- to try out my own ideas?
- to test myself?
- to make a lot of money?
- to be self-reliant?
- to work with congenial people?
- to tackle problems and find solutions?

Think about your responses. Try to rank them in order of personal importance. And consider, then, what is most important to you: recognition? usefulness? money? experience? service? challenge? leadership? independence? These personal motivations, once recognized, can guide your choice of activities, both pre- and post-retirement, on the job and off.

One woman, a manufacturing executive and the first woman to rise so far in her company, recognized her drive for leadership and status. She devoted her post-retirement energies, motivated by the same drive, to securing a long unattainable swimming pool for her hometown. The swimming pool, a highly political issue, had been voted down time and time again; when this woman took the helm she secured townwide approval and private funding as well. She also made a name for herself in the community. She knew exactly what she was doing. Sometimes, of course, people fulfill motivations they do not know they possess. Another executive, a twelve-hour-a-day man who thought that total relaxation was his retirement goal, took up ceramics. His designs were so original, however, and his organizational skills so well-developed, that he wound up running a countywide craftsmen's group. He's working harder than ever.

Each of these people found an individual way, by design or by accident, to satisfy personal needs after retirement. You can do the same, preferably by design. Before you decide on your post-retirement path, however, before you develop your plans for action, map your goals and your objectives. Think through the kind of person you are. Think about the things which have given you most satisfaction in the past. If you like to work with people, you may not be happy alone in a basement workshop, no matter how challenging the project you've tackled; "I couldn't stand the silence—I kept coming upstairs and bothering my wife, until she threw me out of the house." Similarly, if you like the challenge of solving problems, a coin collection may not provide sufficient stimulation. If you want to be free to come and go as you please, escaping a timetable at last, a structured commitment will probably be a mistake. If, on the other hand, you like the security of routine, a totally free and loose existence may leave you restless and unhappy.

Whatever activity or activities you choose, remember that you will have some fifty hours a week after retirement, in addition to the leisure hours you already enjoy. This time may fly, with well-chosen activities, or it may drag. Bowling and bridge may provide sufficient relaxation when you are spending hours at work but may not be expandable, all alone, to fill the extra time. Every single minute needn't be filled, of course; a slower pace is a nice change. Some people really enjoy the rocking-chair approach to retirement. Most truly relish not having to get out of bed on snowy mornings.

But most people need some activity, some activity which is personally meaningful. Most people need a sense of purpose. People need occupation, says gerontologist Alex Comfort, not leisure. Physicians who work in or near retirement communities emphasize the mental and physical deterioration which too often set in when previously purposeful people retire to a mindless round of golf or canasta. When men use exercise to excess, for lack of anything else to do, says one such internist, their whole lives become their bodies; then, when they start to decline in later years, as they inevitably will, they become extremely depressed. Retirees with purpose in their lives, like people of any age who look to the future, are far more likely to remain physically and mentally healthy. Retirees with varied interests are far more likely, too, to remain involved with life, even when one particular interest is ruled out by advancing age or disability.

A great deal depends on the kind of interests you have had all your life and on the kind you set out to develop now, before retirement. "We need continuity in our lives," says Herman Gruber of the American Medical Association. "It's a mistake to think we can take up a completely new activity after retirement, something we've never done before, and find it rewarding. I've never played golf in my life; it would be silly—and defeating for me—to start playing golf at sixty-five. I *am* interested in aging, and will continue to work in the field." If you have a continuing purpose, good. If not, if you've "always wanted to" take up golf or woodworking, to write or to paint, do it now. Don't wait until you "have the time." If you start on a part-time basis now, while you are still working, the transition to full-time will be easy. If you wait until you have retired, it may be more difficult to generate the requisite enthusiasm for a new activity. And if you wait, further-more, retirement itself will continue to hold the fear of the unknown and the untried. People who are not anxious about impending retirement, by and large, are those who know exactly what they plan to do. They have no "unknown" to fear.

MAP YOUR RETIREMENT

To avoid the unknown, take these two steps: decide, now, what you will be doing; and practice before retirement. Take the time to think through your personal goals and to develop objectives and action plans to meet those goals. Take the time to make the decisions that are right for you, take the time to practice, and you will avoid two common retirement traps. You won't be pressured into activities selected by others. Many a retiree has said yes to every volunteer request until there was not a moment of blissful privacy. And you won't pick activities at random, activities that too often prove meaningless, just to fill the time: "I took up stamp collecting because I thought I had to have a hobby, but I'm not interested in stamps."

To make the decision which will be right for you, match what you know about yourself with the options available to you. Acquire as much information as you can, but don't be paralyzed by too much information; decide when enough is enough, and then lend an ear to your own intuition. A lot of intuition is involved in good decision making, Dr. Atchley insists. It's important to be comfortable with decisions you've made, to be comfortable with yourself. When other people start telling you what to do and it sounds rational, but you, for some reason, just keep putting it off, listen to your feelings. The advice may be rational, but not right for you. Be comfortable with past decisions too; don't waste time regretting what might have been. But don't be trapped by past decisions either. It's never too late to make new decisions to meet new needs.

Practice is useful too, and pre-retirement practice of retirement activities can forestall a lot of problems. Practice can be applied to money. Living on a retirement income before retirement is a good way to work out the bugs. Practice can and should be applied to living arrangements. Any move should be preceded by a long vacation-in-residence. And practice can be applied to day-by-day activities. Try "retiring" on weekends for a while. Act as if you're retired, and live the weekend days accordingly. Don't rush to do a week's worth of chores, but do try out some of the hobbies, projects, or activities you are considering as a retirement way of life. Put yourself in the right frame of mind and test your retirement assumptions and alternatives. You'll find out which ones work—and which ones need revision.

Options in Time

4

The Option to Earn

Once upon a time there were three busy men, all of whom relaxed from their labors by making their gardens grow. Then, with the passage of years, all of them retired from the jobs that had kept them so busy for so long. One, a retired engineer, turned his lifelong love of gardening into a second part-time paid-by-the-hour career; he works with a local landscaper during the spring and summer months, advising customers on garden maintenance. One, a motor-vehicle-pool manager, took it upon himself to care for the gardens and shrubbery around his apartment house; he earns no pay but does earn the praise of his neighbors. And one, a textile manufacturer who raised cactus as an avocation, went back to school to learn more about more varieties of this fascinating plant species; he also devotes many hours to the regional cactus club.

Clearly, there are many roads to retirement fulfillment. What do *you* want to do after retirement?

One of your post-retirement options, the one which may be your very first thought, is to keep right on working. Many people do. Many other people think they would like to. Even without financial necessity as a driving force, the momentum built up over forty or more years in the work force is hard to stop. Even thinking about stopping can provoke anxiety.

But is working for pay, on into your sixties and seventies and eighties, the best option for you? Before deciding, take what you've learned about yourself and match it with your personal retirement goals. Will working for pay help you to meet those personal goals? Why do you think you would like to work? Because:

- I can't stand feeling useless.
- I need the money.
- I'll be lonely if I don't.
- It's the best way to stay mentally alert.
- I love the work I do.
- I've got to get out of the house.
- It's the only way to stay healthy.

It's understandable if, at this stage, almost all of these reasons seem valid. But financial need aside (and there are financial costs incurred by working as well, both in actual out-of-pocket expenses and in Social Security limitations), all the other reasons are reasons for staying active, not necessarily for staying at a paying job. We do feel valued when someone offers pay for what we do; we do feel renewed self-respect. Yet more than one retiree has accepted a job he didn't really want, feeling compelled both by the pressures of restricted income and the need for a work-related identity; more than one such retiree has had second thoughts. In accepting a job, Alan H. Olmstead writes, "I had begun to close my new life down and in before it had really had a chance to open up. The warning to all who come after: Don't panic. Don't do anything unless you really want to."

You can keep a sense of usefulness, maintain friendships, and retain mental alertness and physical health through all manner of activities, nonpaid as well as paid. All that's necessary (admittedly, easier said than done) is to shed the Puritan work ethic, shed the notion that worth is measured only in terms of money. You can find usefulness aplenty, for example, in volunteer service, in filling the myriad jobs for which, too often, there is no money. You can also find meaning in personal growth, in long-delayed education, for instance, or newfound creativity. You can find purpose in a combination of activities: volunteer work and a part-time job, or dedication to a craft plus going to school. The options are yours, to select and to combine.

Whatever you decide to do, it should be personally meaningful. Don't be influenced by friends and neighbors. Charlie may have become depressed when he stopped bringing home a paycheck; that has nothing to do with you. Jim, Charlie's neighbor, was happier than ever, with time to devote to his own interests. Evaluate your own goals, your own needs, your own situation. Consider the life-style you have, and the one you want to have. Look at the money you may need. Will extra income provide an extra margin of comfort against inflation? Will it boost your self-esteem more than your standard of living? Or will it be essential for survival? Look at the degree of involvement you prefer. Do you want something that will simply occupy your time? or something that will fully engage your attention as well? Look at the social contact you want. Do you prefer to work or play with others? or alone? And look at the amount of time you want to put in. Do you want to be as busy after retirement as before? Or will you want to change the pace, to have more time to relax?

Give some serious thought to this question of time. Chances are that you won't sleep much later in the morning just because you're retired; you will have the same number of hours in the day. Those hours, from whenever you left for work to whenever you returned at the end of the working day, will be filled, one way or another. When you first retire, there will be a flurry of activity: all the household chores left undone, the papers left unfiled, the letters left unwritten, the books unread. Then, gradually, these activities will be finished or will lose their appeal. What comes next? You still have to fill the hours. They can be filled aimlessly, over the newspaper and at the television set and under your spouse's feet. They can be filled with busywork. They can be filled with purposeful activity. Or they can be balanced, with purposeful activity tempered by well-chosen relaxation. The choice is yours. But make a choice. Don't just fall into one pattern or another.

Whatever your choice, whatever you decide to do, start now. Make your decisions, and your preparations, as far in advance as possible (subject, of course, to change). Make your decisions with the awareness that you have ten to fifteen years to think about, maybe more. Develop goals for those years instead of just living from day to day. Get all the information you can, then be comfortable with your decision; "Don't resist," says Dr. Atchley, "what you're going to do anyway." Follow your inclinations, in other words, but make them well-informed inclinations. Start by looking at all your options: the option to earn, the option to serve, the option for personal growth.

DO YOU WANT TO WORK?

One way to exercise the option to earn is not to retire at all. Despite the decades-old trend toward mandatory retirement at or about age sixty-five, many people still have this option, especially people who are either self-employed or employed by small, unregimented companies. Now, with federal law prohibiting mandatory retirement before the age of seventy, more people will be able to exercise this option. But there is an unanswered question: Will they want to? Will you, given the choice, want to stay in harness? A tentative answer is suggested in the city of Seattle, where mandatory retirement was outlawed on May 9, 1977. Five months later, in October 1977, most of those eligible to retire were still planning to do so. As one Seattle employee put it, "I'm not too hot on working until I drop dead."

The Seattle experience may change as employees have more notice of their option to continue working; those surveyed in mid-

1977 were, for the most part, carrying through on plans made long since. But many men and women, despite this nation's avowed dedication to the work ethic, have had enough by age sixty-five or even sooner. They—you—may be more than ready to trade in the alarm clock for a new life-style.

But there's another way to exercise your option to earn: make a change. Make a change in the work that you do or in the way that you do it or in the time you devote to it. Change jobs if that's what it takes. You can do it at forty and it's called a midlife career change. You can also do it at sixty or sixty-five or seventy, and call it whatever you like. Such a change in career, whether or not you have technically retired from your earlier work, offers new opportunity, opportunity to do what really suits you at a pace that suits you too. It offers revived enthusiasm; even if you have had the best possible job, enthusiasm is likely to wane after forty years. And it offers a fresh start in life, a chance to begin again, with the feeling of youthfulness that beginning entails.

NEW CAREERS

The possibilities for a second career are as broad as your imagination. Your second career can grow directly out of your first career: the insurance executive who becomes an insurance consultant is a prime example; another is the college teacher who edits college texts. It can grow out of an avocation: witness the attorney who turns an interest in photography into a part-time portrait business and the housewife who transforms a passion for genealogy into an advisory service for others. It can grow out of a civic activity: a longtime volunteer for the Girl Scouts was hired to work in the regional Scout Council office; a hospital volunteer is now paid as director of volunteers; another is a patient representative. It can emerge from a hobby: an accomplished weaver is teaching his craft at a regional adult school; a basement carpenter is filing saw blades for other do-it-yourselfers. It can draw on general ability: retirees have second jobs as receptionists, market researchers, census takers. And it can demand new skills, learned after retirement: a former manufacturer's representative, elected to his local library board, went back to school and became a librarian; a high school teacher became a travel agent.

Sometimes a new career takes a twist on an old one. One man turned from a career in medical education to a new career in the education of two-year-olds—and has written a book about this "delightful and stimulating" field. Another man, a specialist in election administration, developed and marketed a new voting device—and spent some post-retirement years as a consultant to the manufacturer. Another, a retired administrator, worked part-time (at different times) doing tax returns with an accountant, organizing office procedures for a local industry, assisting a university comptroller in analyzing the finances of university departments, and acting as auditor for a medical group.

If you are thinking of a new career, try to match your interests and your job opportunities. Don't be locked in by things you've done in the past. Look at your interests and skills with a fresh eye. Remember the occupational threesome: things, symbols, and people. Working with things involves skilled handling and manipulating. If you like to work with your hands, even if you've never done so for pay, you might find post-retirement opportunities in repairing tools or tuning pianos or altering clothes. You might also consider a new field and train, for example, on office machines. An eye for detail and an interest in figures might lead to a position as a cashier or a bookkeeper or a proofreader. Enjoyment of people might point to jobs as receptionist or salesperson, travel agent or information clerk.

Put your interests together. If you particularly like children and you also like to be outdoors, job possibilities include after-school recreation programs and summer-camp and playground positions. If you like the outdoors, but don't particularly want to be with people, try a job as messenger or watchman. If you like people, the indoors, and art, try a job as a museum guide or a position as a lecturer in an adult education class.

FULL-TIME OR PART-TIME?

Your second career can be full-time or it can be part-time. It may involve a long-range commitment, or it may be a temporary assignment; one consultant may have a five-year contract while another may be hired to troubleshoot a particular problem. It may be regular and it may be occasional; many retirees sign up with a temporary agency and work as the spirit—or the pocketbook—moves them. One woman chooses to work two days every week, another prefers to work for two or three weeks and then not at all. Both enjoy the variety of different assignments in different companies. It may be seasonal; one retiree works as business manager of a children's camp while another runs a ski-area concession during the winter months—both have half the year free for travel. It may be as employee—or as employer; many retirees are attracted by the notion of starting their own small business.

Consider your priorities, however, before you make your decision. Would you rather work full-time or part-time? Do you want to play? to engage in other activities? Or are you bored with too much free time? fully alive only when engrossed in work? Have you given yourself a chance to find out? to develop a life outside of work? Consider your basic personality. Do you want the security of a steady job? Or will seasonal or temporary employment suit your need for flexibility and adventure?

Part-time work offers many advantages to the retired, and some disadvantages as well. The workday or week may be shorter, but the hours may not be convenient. Part-time work is often found in businesses that are open for long hours, too long to be staffed by a single shift of full-time employees, such as retail stores, libraries, restaurants, and hospitals. But filling in in these businesses often means working at night and/or on weekends. As a part-time employee, too, you may have to forgo fringe benefits. If you want a vacation, you can take it, but you may not be paid while you are away from the job.

Yet part-time work, especially if you can set your own schedule, is often just right. If you have a skill which others can use, whether or not it stems from your previous career, you can make your own schedule. One woman, an office manager in her pre-retirement incarnation, became a free-lance bookkeeper when she retired, letting local businesses know that she would help organize and keep their books on a per diem basis. She has five clients, each of whom requires a few days each calendar quarter and somewhat more at tax time. She can take on more clients—several local retailers have asked for her services—but prefers to reserve time for traveling. Another retiree, an Illinois man who "always did like to keep records," found a husband-wife job: "We act as bookkeeper at a local club, billing members for their monthly charges, filling out reports and tax statements (many of which we had to learn to fill out), and get paid an amount that lets us keep our Social Security." But bookkeeping is not the only useful skill. Far from it. A retired shop foreman who played the piano for relaxation took lessons in tuning before he retired; he schedules all his tuning appointments in the morning to keep the afternoons free for fishing. Still another, confined to home because of a disability, started a "wake-up" telephone service. Another takes in typing.

If you want to work full-time, whether at your present job or at something new, but prefer the security of working for someone else, remember that your time will continue to be as restricted as ever. "I was offered a full-time job after retirement," a seventy-year-old teacher notes, "but feel that I made the right decision to do only temporary substitute teaching and a little volunteer work. I want time, before I'm too old, to read and garden and enjoy my family."

YOUR OWN BUSINESS

If you want to work full-time, but want to be your own boss, you may be thinking of starting your own business. If so, think hard.

The failure rate of new small businesses is substantial. The toll it can take of you is significant.

Start again by asking yourself some questions. How are you at taking risks? Will the possibility of financial loss, and the likelihood of little time off, keep you up at nights? Or are you challenged and stimulated by the prospect? How are you at assuming responsibility? At keeping track of endless details while keeping the broad picture in mind? How are you at financial management—at securing funds and using them well? How realistic are you at sensing a need and filling it?

Successful small businesses are those that fill a need. If the campers who pour through your town on the way to the nearby state forest have no place to buy supplies, you may have a natural. If there is no local handyman, able and willing to repair small household appliances and workshop equipment, and you have the skill, you may find business flocking to your door. If books and magazines overflow your home after years of collecting, you might try a secondhand book shop—or its latest variation, a book swap shop, where you set a small charge on each transaction to cover overhead costs.

The unifying link to all these successful post-retirement ventures is that they provide a service. And they can start small, often from your own home (just be sure you obey local zoning and business-licensing laws). No major investment in overhead, equipment, or time is necessary. It's the elaborate, expensive ventures—the fully stocked antique shop or ice-cream parlor—that can run into problems. It's also the elaborate ventures that can eat up your retirement time and energy. A nine-to-five job can look like a vacation next to the endless hours often needed to get a new small business under way. And such ventures are expensive as well, often consuming post-retirement income rather than adding to it.

If you are determined, however, and if you are convinced that you have the know-how, the start-up money, and the endurance to make a go of it, do your homework first. Know as much as possible about your product or service before you start, and find out as much as you can about the mechanics of running a business. Consult the Small Business Administration. Their publications and services can be of enormous help. And if you can, work in a similar enterprise before you start your own. The knowledge gained can be invaluable.

YOUR JOB CAMPAIGN: UNDERSTAND WHAT YOU WANT

If, after considering all your options, you plan to continue working, map your job campaign well in advance. Start now, before you retire. First, try to understand what you want most out of your second career: money? a sense of being useful? something to do? stimulation? status? respect? a way to get out of the house? a way to pass the time?

If you are motivated by the wish for status, you may want the recognition of a title in your new career. If you must see the results of your efforts, a specific beginning-to-end job will be best. If you want to try out your own ideas, you may have to be self-employed. If you just want to pass the time, a job without challenge or responsibility, one you can walk away from if you want a vacation, may fill the bill. Think about it. Do you want what you get out of your present job? or something entirely different? The retired insurance executive who set up shop as an independent insurance consultant wanted exactly the same thing—respect for his knowledge in a specialized field, and the status that goes along with that respect. The engineer who went into landscape gardening wanted something entirely different. He wanted to leave a high-pressure job behind and indulge himself in a creative pastime.

YOUR JOB CAMPAIGN: YOUR STRENGTHS AND LIMITATIONS

Picking the right field is important. So is knowing whether you are suited to the field, or to a particular type of job within the field. Do a self-inventory to highlight your strengths and your limitations.

Make a list, first, of all your strengths. Write down all your assets, including not only actual on-the-job experience and educational qualifications, but any and all skills, talents, hobbies, accomplishments. Think about community work you have done over the years. Organizational and/or fund-raising skill developed in volunteer activities can be of great use in the business world. Think about hobbies. Carpentry and collecting and crafts also involve salable skills.

Evaluate your limitations too. Are you dependent on public transportation? Or can you drive to a job in an out-of-the-way location? Do you have family commitments that limit the time you can devote to a job? How is your health? Don't even consider a job that will keep you on your feet all day if you tire easily. Don't try a job that requires close and intense visual work, such as proofreading or bookkeeping, if you are going to feel the strain. The best type of job, if available, is one that offers variety in physical posture and in duties. Then you can avoid both physical and mental fatigue.

YOUR JOB CAMPAIGN: DOING THE GROUNDWORK

Whatever you decide that you want in your second career, do as much groundwork as possible while you are still employed. This removes the urgency, lets you operate from a position of strength. Find out everything you possibly can about the business you want to start or the company you want to join. Take a part-time position, perhaps, to get an inside view—and an inside track. The experience can be positive: "I got a permanent job in department store selling after working part-time in the Christmas rush. I used to work behind a desk, and I love the bustle of the store, love being able to help customers find what they want." The experience can also be negative. But even a negative experience may be positive if it forestalls a serious mistake: "I had a romantic view of running my own bookshop," one sadder-but-wiser book lover remembers. "I thought it would mean I could read a lot and share my knowledge of books with customers. When I actually got a part-time job in a bookstore, however, I found out how little time there is to read and how much time must be spent on paperwork. It's just like running any kind of store. I decided not to get in over my head."

YOUR JOB CAMPAIGN: RÉSUMÉ AND INTERVIEW

When you've completed your self-inventory and decided which field is best, write a new résumé, and brush up your interview skills. The résumé should be organized to highlight your experience and what you have to offer a potential employer; forget the usual chronological arrangement. Instead, describe what you did in terms that really show your ability. Don't write: "Sales manager, Widget Corp., 19– to 19–." Instead write: "As sales manager for the Widget Corp., I supervised a sales staff of fourteen; with innovative sales ideas and a new management system, I increased sales by 42%." Include volunteer experience: "As an organizer of the Community Chest drive, I developed fund-raising techniques which increased the yield by 26%."

Then decide where to send your résumé. Don't be shy. Tell all your friends, relatives, and acquaintances that you are interested in a job, and follow up any leads they may give you. Tell your former employer too (or, better yet, if you are still anticipating retirement, your present employer). You may even be able to stay on, if you want to, on a temporary or per diem basis. Even companies with mandatory retirement regulations often exempt employees under this kind of special arrangement. If you belong to professional or trade associations, clubs or community organizations, share your ambition with your fellow members. Read newspaper classified ads, too, both to sense the demand in your chosen field and to find out average rates of pay. Visit employment agencies, starting with the free services of the State Employment Service in your area and then the private agencies. Just don't sign anything at a private agency and commit yourself to a fee until you decide exactly what you want to do. Take the initiative, too, and write directly to companies that might be able to use your special talents.

Send a résumé along with each letter that you write, and request a personal interview. Keep the letter short; let the résumé, and then the interview itself, tell the story. Prepare for the interview by finding out as much as possible about the company and what it does. The knowledge will give you confidence and will also help you demonstrate just what contribution you can make. At the interview itself, emphasize what you can do for the company, not what you would like the company to do for you. Don't mention your age but, if asked, do stress the positive aspects of your experience and maturity.

At every step of the way, above all else, think positively. It may sound simplistic, but Norman Vincent Peale had the right idea. After all, if you think you're too old to be hired, and go through the motions with a defeatist expression, an employer may well think so too. Be prepared. Know your own abilities. And know the facts about older workers in general.

KNOW THE FACTS

Don't keep on working purely out of fear of the unknown. Consider other options. Give yourself a chance. But if you do decide to keep on earning, don't be put off by myths about older workers. Outright age discrimination is illegal. But attitudes are something else. You may face subtle or not-so-subtle discrimination from employers. Worse, you may be deterred by your own feelings that older workers aren't as desirable as younger ones. There are lots of myths about. But the U.S. Department of Labor provides facts to counter the myths.

Myth: Older workers are too slow; they can't meet production requirements. Fact: Studies show no significant drop in performance and productivity of older workers. Many older workers exceed the average output of younger employees.

Myth: Older workers can't meet the physical demands of

work. Fact: Job analysis indicates that relatively few jobs require great strength and heavy lifting. Laborsaving machinery makes it possible for older workers to handle most jobs without difficulty.

Myth: Older workers aren't dependable; they're absent from work too often. Fact: Workers over 65 have a good record of attendance in comparison with other age groups.

Myth: Older workers are not adaptable; they're hard to train because they can't accept change. Fact: A high proportion of older workers are flexible in accepting change. Adaptability depends on the individual. Many young people are set in their ways, and many older workers adjust to change without difficulty.

Myth: Hiring older workers increases pension and insurance costs. Fact: Pension and insurance costs need not stand in the way of hiring older workers. Costs of group life, accident, and health insurance, and Workmen's Compensation are not materially increased by hiring older workers. Most pension plans provide for benefits related to length of service or earnings, or both. Small additional pension costs, when incurred, are more than offset by the older worker's experience, lower turnover, and quality of work.

There is more than one gap between myth and reality. If you want to work, and are determined, you can probably find a job. The 1974 Harris survey found that 45% of the general public assumed that there were not enough job opportunities for those over 65; only 5% of those over 65 found the lack of job opportunities to be a serious personal problem. First, however, consider your other options.

5

Options for Personal Growth

Although many retirees, close to half according to some studies, continue to earn money after retirement through full-time or part-time or off-and-on employment, not everyone chooses to remain at the beck and call of a paycheck. There are other options. Many people, working for pay or not, find a great deal of satisfaction, a great deal of personal growth, in a wide range of not-for-pay activities in the community and at home. Where the satisfaction is greatest, however, the option is productive. "I said I was finished with responsibilities to others, I just wanted to enjoy myself," one man said. "Then I got talked into helping at a day-care center. Now I know what enjoyment is. It's being needed." And where the satisfaction is greatest, often, the option has been elected before retirement. People who have served as volunteers during their working years continue to do so in retirement. People who have had absorbing hobbies continue to be absorbed. People who have long wanted to return to school seize the opportunity. People who have had no sustaining interest, other than work, more often float aimlessly and unhappily—and resentfully—into the retirement years.

Activity, it seems, begets activity. Active people are ever-active people, absorbed in more than one interest throughout their lives. Substantial numbers of the management-level retirees surveyed by the Conference Board in 1976 are involved in both paid employment and volunteer service. Those who are volunteers are often engaged in more than one pursuit. A seventy-two-year-old New Jersey man, for instance, leads weekly discussion groups among handicapped patients at a hospital for the chronically ill; he is a ham radio enthusiast and member of the International Mission Radio Association, a group of volunteers who put South American missionaries in touch with their families. What's more, he repairs clocks and radios for friends and, in his spare time, does some carpentry. He used to drive for the regional Red Cross unit as well, taking cancer patients to hospitals for treatment, but had to stop because he suffers from emphysema and could no longer help patients from the vehicle and up the stairs. This active man's active wife, also seventy-two, former church organist and choir director, goes with him to the county hospital each week. She started first, in fact, and brought him along. Mrs. W. plays the piano for patient sing-alongs—and thinks of her sometimes frustrating commitment in terms of one patient who chose sing-along time to speak for the first time in years. She, like her husband, leads a busy life, teaching piano part-time, gardening, and raising plants for the yearly church fair.

You may not have been so involved. You may not have had adequate time, during years of earning a living and raising a family, to develop a dormant interest in sculpture or to lead a youth group or to study French or to give time to the local library. But it's not too late. Now you will have time. Now you can embark on all those adventures of exploration and creativity that have tantalized you over the years. Now you can grow, through volunteer service, service to others, and/or through creativity, through voyages of self-discovery.

THE OPTION TO SERVE

There's been some controversy over voluntarism in this country in recent years, sparked by claims that volunteers keep paying jobs away from people who need the income—and by other claims that the only jobs worth doing are worth doing for pay. But there's a long and honorable tradition of volunteer commitment in American life, starting with the cooperative and neighborly barn raisings of Colonial days. This spirit of sharing still permeates many worthwhile activities, large and small, from block-by-block fund raising for the United Way to one-on-one remedial reading help for a neighborhood child.

Older adults are very much a part of this volunteer commitment. Twenty-eight percent of all sixty-five-to-sixty-nine-year-olds, according to the 1974 Harris poll, are involved in volunteer activities. Those with more education and higher income levels are even more involved. The varieties of volunteer opportunities, of course, are virtually limitless. The types which seem to have most appeal for older volunteers, however, are: health and mental health programs, such as working in hospitals or disease prevention clinics; transportation, including driving the aged or the ill to doctors or to shopping; psychological and social support services, such as friendly visitor programs for the homebound or Big Brother or Sister programs for youngsters or outreach programs to find people in need; giveaway programs, such as providing emergency food or staffing charity thrift shops.

As a Volunteer: What Can You Do? Lists of jobs that need filling can be obtained from any local volunteer bureau. One recent list, in a typical suburban township, included requests for volunteers to tutor elementary school children and high school equivalency program adults in remedial English and mathematics, record textbooks for blind children, teach arts and crafts in a mental health center, teach bookkeeping skills, sell merchandise in an elder citizens' craft shop, converse in Greek with a seventy-seven-year-old woman who speaks only Greek. Hospitals have their own lists, running from people to escort patients to X-ray to pharmacists' helpers to information clerks to gift-shop salespeople to library-cart operators. Charities need envelope stuffers and fund raisers;

politicians and causes of all kinds need canvassers and letter writers; civic organizations need members; schools need assistance in the classroom and the library and the playground.

The United States Government has its list, too, of agencies under the ACTION umbrella. If you want a full-time challenge, the Peace Corps (or VISTA, its domestic counterpart) may be for you. The Peace Corps, which trains Americans to serve overseas, requires a two-year commitment. There is no upper age limit, and many volunteers are retirees. A former teacher from Montana became a Peace Corps teacher in Thailand, a former plumber from Pennsylvania taught plumbing in Honduras, a farmer from the Plains states improved agricultural methods among West Africans, and Lillian Carter, who needs no introduction, worked in a family-planning clinic in India. VISTA, Volunteers in Service to America, does much the same thing at home, with 40% of volunteers working in their home communities. A former social worker in Boston directs a telephone referral service in her own neighborhood; volunteers in San Antonio work in consumer and health education; volunteers in Chicago, many both elderly and bilingual, seek out elderly residents of ethnic neighborhoods to tell them about benefits for which they are eligible. VISTA volunteers teach grape-growing techniques, work in mental health centers, conduct neighborhood surveys, establish credit unions, renovate housing, and more, much more.

Both VISTA and the Peace Corps require a major commitment. If you would prefer part-time work in your own community, SCORE or RSVP might be more to your liking. SCORE, the Service Corps of Retired Executives, uses retired business people to counsel struggling small businesses under the auspices of the Small Business Administration. Volunteers meet with owners of new and uncertain business ventures, and pass on their experience in merchandising, record keeping, sales techniques—all the skills that are necessary for business survival. Thus, more small businesses stay afloat, surviving the crucial first five years, while

SCORE volunteers find the assignment a rewarding intellectual challenge.

RSVP, the Retired Senior Volunteer Program, enlists men and women over age sixty, of any background, in a wide range of community-service activities. RSVP has agencies in all fifty states and is locally planned, operated, and controlled. RSVP—its slogan is "You've learned a lot in 60 years of living. Don't keep it to yourself."—can use as much time as you choose to give, in whatever activity you choose. A great deal of care is given, in fact, in matching volunteer with job, and you may, or may not, as you choose, draw on your previous occupational experience. A retired dentist, for example, not at all interested in a suggested assignment doing preventive dentistry in a nursery school, is happily teaching bridge at a senior center instead. RSVP jobs are much like other volunteer jobs, in hospitals and schools, mental health clinics and youth centers. But under RSVP you receive any training which may be necessary for the job, accident and liability insurance are provided, and transportation is arranged if you need it. RSVP also reimburses out-of-pocket expenses in some instances. But don't forget: expenses incurred in any charitable work are tax deductible. If you spend money on telephone calls or postage, uniforms or transportation, keep records of your expenditures to substantiate the deduction.

As a Volunteer: Suit Yourself. There are other agencies and organizations, all eager for your services. You are needed everywhere. But the options are completely up to you. Your choice of commitment should be related to community needs—but even more important, if you're to stick with it, it should be related to your own interests, abilities, and desires, your motivations and your rewards. Some people prefer to do clerical chores and not have to talk to anyone. Others, missing the companionship of work, prefer to be involved with people. Even then, it may take a while to find the right slot. "You can be a 'friendly visitor' in a nursing home," one such volunteer points out, "but it won't work unless you find people to visit who have interests in common. It takes some trial and error." Some people find stuffing envelopes for charity a mindless bore. Others, like a twice-retired ninety-two-year-old Missourian who compiles solicitation kits for Cystic Fibrosis, see it as a worthwhile service as well as a way to keep busy and active. "You always need something important to do," he says, "when you get up in the morning."

Assess your own needs. If you want the structure of an ongoing organization, the security of a niche in the organizational chart, sign up with a large agency or institution. If you want to bypass the risks of whim-directed placement—there may be many assignments you've never heard of, and that you will never hear of if you simply march into the nearest hospital and ask for a job—try the local volunteer bureau or RSVP; a trained interviewer will match you with the job that's right for you. If you want to be creative, however, and assume responsibility for a new project, use your imagination. There are plenty of things that need doing in any community, things that aren't being done.

On the political front, for example, an energetic suburbanite began attending all the meetings of governmental bodies in his community: the town council, planning board, board of adjustment, board of education. He became familiar with their operations, with what they were supposed to do and with what they actually did, and began to speak up, fulfilling what Maggie Kuhn of the Gray Panthers has called a "watchdog" function. Political action—through voting, organizing, and acting as watchdogs—is a way to meet community needs in general and older people's needs in particular in a wide range of areas: housing, economics, consumer protection, health, and so on. Older adults, with more time and a great deal of interest, are playing an increasingly active and important role in the political process. There's more, much more, yet to be done.

And there are other avenues to individual action, other ways of being useful. A housebound retiree, living alone and contemplating what would happen if she fell and couldn't get up, organized a telephone reassurance service, enlisting other volunteers to make telephone calls at specified times to people living alone. If there is no answer, neighbors or relatives are notified. Another retiree, a lifelong book lover, moved to a new housing development and then discovered, to his dismay, that there was no local library. He wound up working, full-time and without pay, starting and staffing a community library. In doing so, of course, he not only fulfilled his own need for books but got to know his new neighbors.

A New Jersey resident, restless after six months of retirement, created the post of patient representative in his local hospital. He makes the rounds each day, holidays included, clipboard in hand, listening to patient complaints. Another man was asked by a neighbor, a high school teacher, to share his woodworking skills with the shop class. The students responded positively, he enjoyed the experience himself, and so he started a talent pool to coordinate the needs of the schools with locally available talent. Under the auspices of this volunteer-run group other volunteers speak of their travels, help in language classes, demonstrate crafts, explain their careers. Along somewhat similar lines, a retired Virginian organized a community exchange of useful services; he maintains files of available skills—from sewing to gutter cleaning to house-plant tending to plumbing—and puts residents needing services in touch with those who can provide them. Hours are debited and credited, so that services owed one neighbor can be paid off to another.

Look at your community and determine what needs to be done. Look at yourself and see what you have to offer. As a volunteer, all the options are yours. You can work with people or work alone; you can help the young or the old; you can assist the sick or the well. Select your purpose first: the charity or organization or agency or group whose goals you wish to further. Then choose your method. You can work for almost any purpose in many ways: on an advisory board, raising funds, stuffing envelopes, giving speeches, soliciting members, maintaining files—and working directly with people, providing the help they need.

As a Volunteer: Be Professional. Finding the right job is crucial. So is being professional in your performance of that job. Let the agency know when they can expect you—and be there at that time. If your time will be erratic, because you plan to travel frequently, tell them so, in advance, so they can plan accordingly. There are jobs that can be done on an erratic basis, but there are others that require regular attendance if trained personnel are not to lose valuable time. In return for your commitment, you have the right to be treated as a professional. A "volunteer's bill of rights" is set forth in Julietta K. Arthur's *Retire to Action:*

1. You have a right to ask for a suitable assignment and to expect consideration to be given your preferences, your temperament, your education, and your experience.
2. You have a right to be given information in advance, about the organization you are joining, its policies, its programs, and its objectives.
3. You have a right to know where and when you will work and be assigned in an orderly way to some place that fits the job you will be doing.
4. You have a right to expect to have an orientation session, and if necessary, a training period.
5. You have the right to guidance and direction by some person assigned to invest time in giving it.
6. You have the right to expect to engage in a variety of experiences if you are able to execute them when they arise.
7. You have the right to know about any new developments in the organization which may give you a chance to expand your services.
8. You have a right to continuing education if you prove worthy of it, for greater responsibilities.

9. You have the right to be heard by some person in authority if you have queries or complaints.
10. You have a right to be treated as a bona fide co-worker of the regular staff, regardless of the fact that you are not receiving a salary.

With all these rights, what will you get out of being a volunteer? Exactly what you would get out of a well-chosen paying job, minus the pay. Some find even more. A retiree in South Carolina, actively involved in his local Council on the Aging and in a Meals on Wheels program, puts it this way: "In my own experience, the little I do in volunteer work brings me greater rewards than any check I ever cashed. I am just as busy as I ever was and with greater satisfaction." The men surveyed by the Conference Board, many of whom were engaged after retirement in both work-for-pay and volunteer work, cited these advantages: enjoyment of the work itself, maintaining contact with other people, being able to use knowledge and skills developed during the earlier career, the chance to develop new knowledge and skills. Overwhelmingly—83% of those surveyed—they cited the sense of doing something worthwhile; interestingly, of those working for pay, and citing the same advantages, only 59% referred to that sense of doing something worthwhile.

Don't expect tangible rewards, however, and don't expect to be thanked by the recipients of your bounty. "Don't expect people to be grateful," one volunteer warns. "You can get very irritated if you wait for a 'thank you.' But it's worth doing, if you find the right job, because it's a challenge and because it's fun." The rewards are intangible but they are real. A well-chosen volunteer commitment can help you to meet the personal goals you've set for yourself. It can help you to achieve recognition, find friends, maintain status, expand your knowledge and skills, apply your talents, work with your hands or with your head, find stimulation and excitement and variety in life. It can help you to remain in control of your own life, solve your own problems. It can help you to have an impact on your community, and on the world. It can help you find and keep a sense of being worthwhile through doing something worthwhile.

Don't be like the Indiana man, a retired steel-mill clerk, who, bitter about forced retirement, has retreated into a shell. "I spend a great deal of time now just reading and watching TV," he says. "I am getting awfully fed up with this and don't feel like doing anything else. After all, they have almost convinced me that I am through, washed up, and not capable of doing anything more. I feel like such a waste." This attitude is a waste, when there's so much to be done, so much that you can do and feel good about doing. And volunteers, those who find a personally meaningful commitment, do feel good. Look at the former printer who devotes two days a week to a hospital, doing "everything that needs to be done, from changing beds and running samples to the lab to feeding patients." Above all, according to the hospital administration, he spreads good cheer. And he reaps some good cheer himself. As he puts it: "Listen, I'm a little guy; I'm five feet five. But when I walk out of here at the end of the day, I feel ten feet tall."

THE CREATIVE OPTION

There's more than one way to skin a cat, as the saying goes, and more than one way to remain active and involved. People who are absorbed in a creative effort, of any kind, are people who continue to grow. Some people talk about hobbies, recommend them to the retired. There's nothing wrong with hobbies—except that some of them are little more than mindless busywork, unenthusiastically adopted as time killers—but I prefer to include meaningful hobbies, those that provide real growth and real fulfillment, under the heading of creativity.

All sorts of things are creative, all sorts of things provide ongoing opportunity for personal growth. The best are those which reflect your own personality and those which can change and expand to meet your changing needs and interests. The best, again, are those chosen early in life—but some enormously successful interests have emerged late in life when people, at last, have time for themselves. The best, whenever chosen, are those broad enough and deep enough to keep you involved over time.

A note of caution, from an eighty-year-old midwesterner: "Don't count on your stamp collection to keep you busy if you have neglected it when you were working. In general, this kind of thing will have less appeal as a time filler than it had when minutes were snatched from sleep. There's more hope in new crafts and skills related to some new central purpose." But it depends, of course, on you—and on the activity you choose. One man returned to the piano, untouched for sixty years, and practiced two hours a day until proficiency returned. A woman who never had time until retirement for long-coveted dancing lessons is busily doing folk, social, and belly dancing at the age of sixty-nine. A New Englander took up weaving to join his wife in an engrossing hobby; he found working at the loom a challenging respite from day-to-day responsibilities as a college administrator. Later, in retirement, he and his wife continued weaving for their own pleasure, traveled the world in search of new techniques and ideas, and exhibited in crafts shows up and down the eastern seaboard. Absorbed in creativity, they were never bored, never gave up on life.

Choosing an Art, a Craft, an Activity. What about you? You've ruled out working for a paycheck, or working without. Or you are working, either way, but have more time and energy. All right, what do you want to do? Not what do you think you should do, or what do others suggest you do, but what do you want to do? Don't pick a hobby out of a cocked hat, if you want it to have any meaning for you. Apply the same criteria that you apply to choosing a paying or volunteer job, and select a creative option that will use your talents, satisfy your motivations, and provide rewards. Select an activity that will demand an investment of mental and/or physical energy, one that will keep you on your toes by requiring new learning, one that provides a challenge.

You may have a long-standing interest which can be developed. "For years I had taken along a sketch pad and paints on trips," one woman recalls, "but I found myself lacking in the skills and knowledge to develop a picture. I attended night classes . . . I read books on art, and visited museums . . . I became interested in watercolor and took a course in that. . . ."

You may be looking for a new interest, and there are a host of possibilities. Some are active, some passive; some are solitary, and others are companionable. Many can be one or the other, at different times and to meet different needs. Collecting, one of the most popular of pastimes, may be a desultory time killer for someone who does it because there is nothing better to do—and an absorbing passion for someone who pursues a historical interest through collecting, who joins a club, or who transmits his passion through teaching others. Collecting may be solitary, in the hours spent in organization; it may be companionable and lead to new friendships through shared interests. Collecting may be a sedentary activity, pursued by catalog in the comfort of one's home. And it may be active, as the quest for particular treasures leads to flea markets and galleries, fairs and shops.

Anything and everything can be collected: stamps and coins, of course, plus postcards and political memorabilia, matchbook covers and glass bottles, antique tools and military miniatures, autographs and posters. Your particular collection may develop during vacation travels. One family started a collection of postcards from every place they visited over the years, then turned to old postcards as well. It may stem from another hobby. An architect who does cabinetry at home picked up a set of old-fashioned wooden clamps while browsing in a secondhand store. They worked so well that he picked up a massive plane on another excursion. Now he seeks old but functional tools wherever he goes. And a collection may develop out of your occupation. A tobacco sales manager, for instance, engrossed with tobacco memorabilia, collects plug cutters, tin identification tags, advertisements, and containers from the turn of the century. He and his wife frequently pack a picnic lunch and visit flea markets; she looks for antique kitchen implements while he ferrets out more tobacco cutters. Home again, he disassembles, sandblasts, reassembles, and repaints the cutters. He meets with other collectors to trade stories and, occasionally, cutters, and he has become so involved that he visited the Smithsonian Institution in Washington for historical research on the tobacco industry. Any hobby this intense is a creative pastime.

The arts are creative, of course. So are crafts. If you have any skill with your hands, any eye for color and shape and form, you may be fascinated by ceramics or stained glass, enameling or sand painting, puppet making or basketry, batik or jewelry design, sculpture or macrame or decoupage or calligraphy. You can make candles, bake bread, tailor a suit, plant a garden. A retired merchant seaman spends long hours building lovingly detailed models of sailing ships, models which he occasionally exhibits at libraries and fairs. He began after retirement. A doctor works an hour or two a day, for about three months at a time, assembling a gas-powered and electronically directed model boat, then joins other enthusiasts for afternoons of putting boats through their paces. He is still working but puts in more time on his boats as he winds down his professional obligations.

A reading program, personally planned around a subject of interest, is also creative. Are you fascinated by Greek history? excited by archaeology? challenged by military strategy? Go it alone, with guidance, if you like, from your local librarian. Even reading can be companionable, can lead to new friendships and mental growth, if you join with others for discussion; try an established Great Books club, or a library discussion group, or form a neighborly reading circle for informal but lively talk.

Photography is a creative pursuit with many byways, in taking pictures alone or in taking and developing them. You might build a family pictorial history, for instance, by combining organized and labeled pictures from the past (now is the time to go through all those old shoeboxes, now is the time to attach names to all those faces) with a contemporary account of day-to-day life. Shoot pictures throughout a day of ordinary living—of eating breakfast, getting the paper, working in the garden, chatting with neighbors—for an intimate portrait of your family. Construct a family tree through a combination of photographs and written text, and share it with your grandchildren.

Get involved in the outdoors, through hiking or nature study or birding, through solitary or companionable pursuits, as you choose. One interest can lead to another. "I started backpacking with my sons," an industrial researcher in New York explains. "Then I became interested in the trees I was seeing on these expeditions. I began to learn about trees, to be able to identify them in different seasons. That led me into curiosity about the succession of tree types in forests, and I started doing some research. Now, since my wife gave me a camera, I'm getting into nature photography. There isn't time enough for everything I want to do."

People who "never have enough time for everything there is to do" are people who are "turned on" by life, who are mentally active and energetic to the very end of life. A creative pastime can do the same for you, whether you bring it with you into retirement or develop a new one after retirement. It's never too late to get started. But you must be willing to invest some time and effort, to find out all you can about the various possibilities. You may have to sample a few pursuits before you find the one that is best for you. How do you begin? For starters, look at the nearest well-stocked newsstand or paperback bookstore; it is lined with craft and hobby and special-interest publications of all kinds. Visit your local library, and make good use of its extensive resources. Join a club at your town's recreation department or the nearest community center. Take a course.

THE OPTION TO LEARN

Taking courses, going to school, can be a good way to find out about creative possibilities of various kinds. It can also be a creative pursuit in itself, a path toward personal growth. Many older adults are returning to school, for a host of reasons. Practical need is one reason. "Without that course in home maintenance, I never could have made it on my pension." Leisure interest is another. Courses in bridge and ballroom dancing and woodworking are offered everywhere—and filled by people with time on their hands. Desire for a degree is another reason. Many retirees never had time to go to college in earlier years, and they relish the opportunity now. Vocational interest is a reason: "I have to leave my store manager's job at sixty-five, but with some courses in accounting I'm going to have a second career." And pure intellectual interest is a reason too. Adult men and women are filling the rosters of courses in music and French and political science.

If you're motivated to learn, for any of these reasons or for reasons of your own, your only problem may be one of where to go—not because few places welcome older students, but because so many do. Colleges and universities, faced with declining birthrates and fewer students of traditional college age, are rolling out the welcome mat for adults of all ages. Two-year community colleges, designed to meet local needs with low-cost educational programs, have both credit and not-for-credit courses of all kinds. Special-interest courses for adults are also found in community centers, high schools (usually in the evening), Y's, libraries, museums, churches, and synagogues. Even the housebound can benefit; correspondence courses provide the opportunity to study at home.

Learning: No Degree Necessary. If you're not interested in a degree, your program choices are almost endless. In addition to all the day and evening adult courses in your own community, in everything from auto mechanics to world affairs, there are week-end trips and summer "education vacations" and short residential programs ranging from a few days to several weeks. Some courses meet on a college campus, others in wilderness settings. Few require any educational prerequisites, other than interest. Fees are usually reasonable. Most of the students are usually adults. If you want to mix with younger students and take regular semester-long courses in a college setting, often very expensive, you may find that your age entitles you to a reduction in fee. Sometimes, where space is available, there is no charge at all. Some institutions charge a fee if a course is taken for credit, but do not charge if the same course is taken on a not-for-credit basis. You will have to match your interests, and your reasons for returning to school, with what is available in your vicinity.

Learning: If You Want a Degree. If you're eager for a degree, however, you don't necessarily have to attend college for four years. You don't necessarily have to set foot on a college campus. There are a number of innovative approaches available today, designed to pave the way for students above "normal" college age. One such program is CLEP, the College Level Examination Program, which enables you to take examinations and receive college credit, based on the results of the exams, for learning which takes place outside of school. If you've learned Spanish through travel or data processing on the job or American literature through reading for pleasure, you can take a CLEP exam for possible credit. More than 1,500 colleges and universities currently grant advanced placement on the basis of CLEP exams. The General Educational Development (GED) tests offer a high school diploma by examination in a similar fashion. And some institutions will award a high school diploma for course work completed on the road to a college degree. Don't let the lack of previous formal education stand in your way. There are so many older adults whose schooling was cut short by other responsibilities that (1) you are far from alone and (2) all kinds of special provisions are being made to formally recognize your lifelong learning.

One such provision is the state-sponsored external degree programs in New York, New Jersey, and Connecticut (but open to residents of any state), which grant degrees to adults on the basis of supervised independent study. They, too, grant credit for "life experience," the documented skills you've gained in years on the job and in the community and at home. Some private institutions, such as Goddard College in Vermont and Stephens College in Missouri, also offer a degree through a combination of independent study at home, life experience, and some supervised seminars. There are also college courses given by mail, by the sixty-eight universities which are part of the National University Extension Association.

Schooling, any schooling, offers a challenge. It offers even more of a challenge when you've been away from academic discipline for many years. It also offers rewards. It can be rewarding to learn watercolor techniques in an evening adult workshop. It can be mind stretching to tackle anthropology with a seemingly razor-sharp group of college students. Mental stimulation comes from study of all kinds—and it may require more discipline and more work to study via correspondence or under an external degree program—but the give and take of a classroom setting where minds come into conflict, especially with students of different ages, is a rejuvenating experience.

Learning: You're Never Too Old. Some 480,000 people over 65 are enrolled in some kind of educational program. Many more people would like to enroll but are reluctant. "I'm interested in world affairs, international relations," one suburbanite in his seventies noted, "and the local college has reduced admission fees for people over sixty-two. But I don't know. I don't think I can learn any more. After all, you can't teach an old dog new tricks." Not so. I don't know about dogs, but it's not so with respect to humans. Substantial research indicates that people can learn all through life, as long as they are motivated to do so. "I would firmly state that one is never too old to learn," says Paul B. Baltes, professor of human development at Pennsylvania State University. "The question is what you want to learn. . . ."

Age itself does not reduce the capacity to learn, although ill health may do so. The older learner may actually be a better learner, with levels of experience that make learning meaningful.

Intelligence levels are as high among older people, with the same wide range of individual differences as among younger people. The younger generation is just closer to formal study and may have had more of it. College is commonplace these days, as it was not for those who fought the Depression. But the gray matter is still there, bolstered by experience; you know what's worth learning and can learn it well. It may take a bit longer, as you get older, to learn some things. It may be harder to remember newly learned material. But this is because, simply stated, you already have so much in storage. The problem is not in remembering, Dr. Baltes points out, but in keeping past memory, chock-full of lifelong learning, from interfering with new things you want to remember. The problem may not be in memory at all, in fact, but in the process of learning itself. If your study skills are rusty or your hearing not quite what it ought to be or if you're trying to learn too much too fast, you may fall behind. Take a deep breath if this happens to you; try a new approach to studying—reading aloud, perhaps, or going over notes with a classmate—and give yourself plenty of time. Take a course in study skills if you feel it will help. Don't be embarrassed. It's probably been a long while since you embarked on a formal course of study. But you've been learning for a lifetime; you have the capacity. Look at the revolutionary social changes you've lived through and adapted to, look at how you've learned to cope with changes in your own life—not formal learning, perhaps, but learning nonetheless. You can tackle formal learning too, and enjoy it, if you want to.

It's worth a try. Staying active keeps you involved in life, and while there may come a time when you can't be as physically active as you would like, no one (no one but you) can stop you from being mentally active. The rewards are many: mental stimulation, self-respect ("I did it!"), challenge, and not least, the opportunity to meet people with similar interests, people of all ages.

This last benefit, meeting people of all ages, being thrown in with youngsters, doesn't always look like a benefit at first glance. Some older adults are reluctant to enroll in on-campus courses, feeling uncomfortable at the prospect of mingling with the young. If this is true of you, use what psychologist Frances Stern calls "the power of positive daydreaming." Picture yourself in a classroom, as the only "grown-up" among a roomful of teen-agers. What's the worst thing that could possibly happen? They might ignore you. You might be uncomfortable. Then what? You can always quit if things don't improve. Or you can concentrate on your studies and ignore your classmates. But what's the best thing that could happen, if you stick it out, if you give the kids—and yourself—a chance? You'll probably stretch your mental muscles. And you may even reach across the generation gap. The younger students are sometimes uncomfortable too, not quite sure how to respond to the older adult, not quite sure how *they* look to you. But rapport doesn't usually take long. "They had to observe me for a bit," one seventy-eight-year-old music student recalls. "Then, finally, they decided that I still have all my marbles. Now we're friends. I have one good friend in class, in fact, who's twenty years old. She's younger than my granddaughter. It's nice."

Meeting new friends is nice. So is self-fulfillment. So is growth. Personal growth, through whatever path suits your needs and your tastes, can keep you young. You will probably find, in fact, as so many others have, that involvement in one activity leads to involvement in another. You may take a course to learn a creative craft, and learn it so well that you end up teaching it to others. You may find that volunteer service leads to a new interest, one explored through returning to school. The permutations and combinations are as varied as your own interests. But pursuing your interests, whatever they are, will keep you growing, keep you involved in life.

Options in Space

6

To Move
or Not to Move

Ellye and John L. sold their Ohio home when John retired, and moved to an adult community in Arizona. The climate was pleasant, they found, and the community lived up to its advance billing. But the pull of family and of old friends was too strong. Within a year they moved back to Ohio.

Marie and Ed S., on the other hand, moved to a retirement village while Ed was still working. The village, only an hour's drive south of their former New Jersey home, allowed easy access to work, and to family and friends. Ed has enjoyed the village on weekends for several years, while Marie, who retired earlier, enjoys its range of activities on a full-time basis. They have every intention of staying put.

Ann T., a teacher, determined to remain in the college town where she had lived for years, with access to the library, to cultural events, and to former colleagues. She likes her apartment and has no intention of moving at all—although the harshest winter months may tempt her to travel.

Alice and Tim K. looked forward to retirement because, at last, they could move halfway across the country to live near their only daughter. They did move—and found their daughter and her family busy with their own lives, their own friends. The family that went all out to entertain them on a two-week visit could not do so on a permanent basis. Alice and Tim had to begin to make their own friends, mold their own new life in new surroundings.

Betsy and Ken N., however, want nothing more than to stay in their comfortable home, near longtime neighbors, in the community in which they feel they belong. The house, comfortable though it is, and full of memories, is large for two people and increasingly a nuisance to maintain. Ken once enjoyed puttering around—but he no longer feels like getting up on a ladder to clean the gutters or getting down under the sink to repair some balky plumbing. And it isn't easy to find people to do small jobs. The N.'s are beginning to feel that they may have to move.

SHOULD YOU MOVE?

To move or not to move, that is the first question. And if to move, where to—that is the second. Most real-life retirees, despite the stories you've heard, do not move. Most stay in the communities, and the houses, they've known and enjoyed for years. But most probably do give moving at least a passing thought. You may think about moving if:

- your children live far away.
- you only moved here in the first place because it was convenient to work.
- your neighborhood is changing.
- your house seems awfully big for two people.
- house maintenance is beginning to become a pain in the neck.
- the climate *must* be better elsewhere.
- you'd like to return to earlier roots.
- an all-activities-in-one-place adult community seems more and more attractive the longer you think about it.
- retirement seems a good time for a fresh start.

You may, however, want to think twice:

- Your children may live far away, but your son's company may transfer him every few years. Your children may live far away, but in a community or with a life-style that does not appeal to you. They may urge you to come, to take an apartment near them, to be in close touch with your grand-children, and the thought may tempt. But think carefully. "If we yield to their pressure," writes Avis D. Carlson, "we will have to rely on them emotionally because it may be too late to build a place for ourselves in a new community. Can we weather this drop in status? Or will we fall swiftly into dependent old age?"

- You may have moved here because it was convenient to work. But that was some years ago, and now this place is home. You may not notice your roots, until you try to pull them up, but they are there. Your neighborhood may be changing, but change is sometimes for the better. The new people may be interesting, if more diversified, than the old residents, the new shops more fun.

- Your house may seem awfully big for two people, and the maintenance is becoming a chore—but it's just big enough to hold a lot of memories (to say nothing of visiting grand-children), and the youngster next door is big enough and willing enough to help out. Anyway, the house is paid for, and there's no more mortgage—although one can't deny that property taxes are rising inexorably.

- Your childhood roots may exert a strong pull, but be sure that they're still where you left them. Nostalgia may blur reality, and communities have a way of changing. "I moved from the city in which I had been teaching for thirty-five years, back to the city in which I had grown up. It turned out to be a greater change than I had expected due to the development of the city. Old landmarks had gone, and various monstrosities had taken their place. Old friends were no longer there, and to a certain degree it was like moving into a strange city."

• The climate may be better elsewhere, but you might really miss changing seasons, the autumn colors, the tingle of winter. You might find year-round heat not only boring but a burden. A librarian who moved from New York to Florida planned carefully, including visits to Florida at many times of the year. The summer heat, nonetheless, was an unpleasant surprise. "Even though I had gone to Florida for more than twenty years, including many trips during the year, we had not expected the heat to linger so long . . . with air conditioning and if a person likes to stay indoors this is fine, but I love the outside."

It isn't only southern heat that can be deceptive. Any climate for which one is unprepared can have a depressing impact. One couple moved to San Francisco and loved it for several months. Then the weather changed. "Presently, the days shortened, the morning fogs in the city lingered longer, the evening fogs rolled in over the hills earlier and stayed later, our apartment grew chilly and chillier, our coughing grew deeper, the doctors we consulted seemed as hurried and distant and perfunctory as emergency-room interns, the streets on rainy nights seemed darker and more menacing and became windier and colder. We took to phoning nearby markets and having our food sent to our apartment COD, we spent more and more of our days and nights holed up there, swathed in blankets and yearning to be home again. When, at long last, we got back here, we reveled in our old familiar surroundings and for months had a marvelous time matching rueful stories with old familiar friends who had sojourned in Florida or Southern California or Colorado or Mexico or that place in Arizona where a London bridge has been moved stone by stone. And with them we chorused, 'Never again.' "

San Francisco, of course, is lovely. So is Southern California and Florida and Colorado. But for many people, unfamiliar weather patterns coupled with unfamiliar surroundings add up to misery. "Home is where you were born," is the way one native of Michigan puts it. "If you were born in ten feet of snow, that's home."

- Retirement communities seem attractive—new and fresh, filled with people like yourself—but you're not sure life wouldn't be just the least bit dull. Do you really want to live in a community where everyone is about the same age, with the same interests in life, and all the interests centered right there in the community? Would you find it secure? or stultifying? Retirement seems a good time for a fresh start, and indeed it is, but why not make a fresh start at home, bolstered by familiar places and familiar people?

WHAT IS HOME?

Maybe the real first question is, What is home? Home is many things to many people, but to most, it is as much a psychological space as it is a physical space. Home is an extension of personality. Home is where you are in control. Home is where you can relax, let down your hair, be yourself. Home is familiar ground, filled with familiar possessions. Home is a familiar community, filled with dear friends. Home is where the heart is.

Home, to one, is wherever the family is. "I've moved fourteen times in my married life; every time the children were settled in school and I felt at home in the community, the company asked us to move. I've learned to make a home out of any house. So we might just as well find a retirement spot that suits us. We have no particular ties here." Home, to another, is a complex mosaic made up of family and friends and neighborhood and the physical presence of a long-lived-in house itself. "I couldn't think of moving. My roots have been in this community for twenty-seven years. We've poured so much energy into this house over the years, so much devotion, to make it just right."

You can live anywhere after retirement, at least in theory. In fact, of course, there are many considerations that dictate your decision, considerations both practical and psychological. What will your finances permit? Can you afford to give up a paid-up home and assume a new mortgage? Can you afford to stay in a house that gets more expensive to maintain with each passing year? Do you want to stay? Or do you have itchy feet and, at last, a chance to satisfy the itch?

Think about it. What do you like about your present home and its surroundings? The view from the breakfast-room window? the friendly neighbors? the accessibility of shopping? the living-room fireplace, to sit around on wintry nights? the tree you planted when your first daughter was born? the old-fashioned formality of parlor and drawing room? or the easy informality of rooms that flow into one another? Alan H. Olmstead, writing just after his retirement about the many ways in which their house was made a home—the trees they planted, the floors they stained—concludes:

> This is the house of our Christmases and our Thanksgivings, the house to which our children came home, with new friends, from their first semesters in college, the house which could open out for our good times and provide suffering corners for our moments of pain. It is also, of course, the house which is beginning to need to be shingled again, even though we told ourselves, when we selected expensive wood shingles thirteen years ago, that that was probably the last roof we would have to pay for. Its vast outer surface will soon be asking for fresh paint. Its interior pipes grow porous; the cost of heat escalates every winter; there really is no hard-boiled statistical way of proving that we can afford to stay here and keep the place livable. But move into something smaller and less expensive and easier to maintain? Only, in present mood, as a dead body.

Sentimental? Yes. But why not be sentimental about a home, if you have one, that has sheltered your family for years? Why not, if possible, let your heart rule your head? These are the years that belong to you. So jot down your own thoughts. Make your own list of tangible and intangible advantages in your present residence, and rank the advantages in order of their importance to you. Then, in any considered move, be sure that your new location will provide similar satisfactions.

Both people and places are important in most lists; familiar people and familiar places provide continuity, keep most retirees from moving very far, if at all. If you do move, you may miss old friends most of all. You can, of course, make new friends, but will friendships based on shared experiences of the present replace those of a lifetime? You may also want to consider, in advance, whether you are the kind of person who can make new friends easily. How outgoing are you? How willing to take the first step? How interested?

WHERE TO MOVE

The answers to these questions may determine whether you move at all. They may also influence your decision about where to move. If you choose a community in which everyone is new, such as a retirement or "adult" village, making friends may be easier. You may be swept right into a whirl of community activities. Everyone is in the same boat in these communities, both in terms of being a new resident and in terms of sharing a leisure-oriented life-style. If you move to an established community, making friends may be more difficult, unless (1) you are outgoing and willing to make a deliberate effort to join organizations and meet people and/or (2) you already have friends or organizational ties to ease the way.

Sometimes, of course, the best-thought-out plans are undermined. One couple invested considerable time and energy in selecting where they would live, settling on a small university town where they had once lived and where they still had friends. When the wife, at fifty-nine, had a heart attack, the criteria were revised; then, the husband writes, "We looked for level ground for walking, an equable climate, and little wind. Our selection has proved to be a good one, but we have found that the person who enters at retirement a community where he has no standing has to work at the job to build up a circle of friends. . . . Through professional associates whom I have known earlier and through a few organizations, I have been able to start a new life, with a few close friends, but my wife and I think that we would have had an easier time of it had we stayed with our first love and gone back to the small university community."

In missing old friends and associates, as this retiree found, you may even miss part of your own identity, the "self" built up in others' eyes over the years. You may have been a great fund raiser for the local volunteer ambulance corps or an organizer of church suppers. You may have supplied the neighbors with home-grown beefsteak tomatoes or been known as the person who could fix anything. No one in a new community will know any of this. No one in a new community will know what you can, or can't, do. You will have to make a new reputation for yourself.

This can be a grand opportunity to start over if you like, to portray yourself in a totally new light. Maybe you've always meant to be more involved in the community but people gave up calling you because you were always too busy. You could, of course, let people know you're available now, but if you move you can start with a fresh slate, without apologies for the past. If you move, you can even gloss the past a little, one writer suggests, and if such things matter to you, upgrade your standing in society. Say that you've had a supervisory position or been in management—and who's to know that you were only a cog in the corporate wheel? You can also turn the reputation business upside down. One former executive wanted to sit back and relax, without living up to anybody's preconceived notions about his "place" in the community. "I've done my share of fund raising and board sitting," is the way he puts it, "and I've had enough. So we moved and when people asked what I'd done, I just let on that I was 'with' such and such a corporation. I didn't bother to say I'd been a vice-president. No one cares anyway."

There are advantages to making a new reputation, to creating the image that suits you. But as many people find, there are also built-in disadvantages. When no one knows you, you have to explain yourself, and you may not want to. "The club at church wanted someone to run the fair. They didn't ask me, of course, because I'm new. But I ran the fair every year back home." You have to show what you can do, and you may not have the energy or inclination to become overly involved. "People in the new community don't know what a great guy I am," one midwesterner commented ruefully, "and I'm not the kind who can tell them. They don't care, which is maybe even worse!"

If you decide to move, moreover, you may miss the providers of neighborhood services which you took for granted: the doctor and dentist who took care of you for years, who knew your tolerance for pain and knew when something was really wrong; the butcher who knew your preferences—and your budget— without being told; the traffic policeman who waved a morning salute; the paper boy who put the paper just where you wanted it; the auto mechanic you would trust with your car. It may have taken years to establish such relationships; how do you feel about establishing replacements?

And if you do move, you may also miss familiar places, places filled with memories—not just your home itself but the park you crossed each day on the way to work, the recreation center open at convenient hours, the tree-lined streets in your old neighborhood. Pangs of nostalgia can be unexpected. If you make a drastic change in your surroundings, even for the better, the pangs can be severe: the transplanted urbanite misses the bustle of the city at the same time that he relishes the relative security of the countryside; the former exurbanite misses the tranquility of his old surroundings while enjoying the convenience of city facilities. Even a move from suburb to suburb, however, is a change of place. One couple who made such a move loved their new surroundings and never regretted the move. But they did, every once in a while, miss familiar stores; they found solace in visiting the local Sears, finding that "they look the same" in Michigan and in California.

AND IF YOU DON'T MOVE?

Moving may pose problems. But staying put is not necessarily the answer. There are undoubtedly disadvantages as well as advantages to your present location. Has peace and quiet been replaced by heavy traffic? Has an influx of young families raised property taxes beyond belief? Has the park you loved, the one next door that was a recognized if unlabeled bird sanctuary, made way for a sorely needed school? Has air pollution affected your garden? Has your urban neighborhood deteriorated, and the crime rate risen? Or is your rural home as peaceful and quiet and lovely as ever, but far too isolated for your present peace of mind? Have the stairs which once provided a needed buffer between children and adults become a burden to climb on a daily basis? Is the driveway too long to shovel? Evaluate the disadvantages of your present location and, if you do decide to move, be sure to replace them with advantages.

Staying put is not always the answer even in terms of human relationships. You may stay, and others may go. Children relocate; old friends move to warmer climates; the old family doctor is replaced by a young group of doctors; your dentist retires; even the paper boy grows up and is replaced—by one who refuses to deliver the paper right to your door. The effect of these changes is cumulative, not the all-in-one wrench that occurs when you move, but the effect is felt.

What's worse, your own identity may shift, even on home ground. If you have felt that your status, whatever it was, stemmed from your occupation, you may feel that your status changes with retirement. If your contact point with neighbors revolved around a commuter's timetable, you may feel distinctly ill at ease on weekday afternoons—especially in a child-oriented suburban world. If you have based your status on a certain life-style, which you can no longer afford to maintain, you may feel embarrassed. If such things bother you, it may be time to move.

You must make your own decision about whether or not to move. No one else can make it for you (although well-meaning friends and relatives may try). It's not an easy decision, since practical elements are submerged into feelings, but there are some guidelines: determine your priorities, consider all the alternatives, and communicate with the people in your life.

DETERMINE YOUR PRIORITIES

Think about the goals you've set for your retirement years, and evaluate them in terms of where they can best be fulfilled. Is a comfortable way of life most important to you, an easy life in a moderate climate? Many older people do move to the sun belt in quest of the good life. Many find it. But one study also found that as time progressed, urban conveniences become more important than climate. People in a self-contained Southern California desert community were not as happy, by and large, as those closer to a metropolitan center. The desert community was only ten minutes by car from a major city—but for those who could no longer drive, ten minutes might just as well have been ten hours.

Are economic considerations most important? Then you have to be hardheaded and practical. Take out pencil and paper and figure out exactly what your present residence costs to maintain. Compare those costs to the maintenance of a new residence, remembering that moving itself is a costly proposition. The moving men are only the initial cost. You must also consider closing costs and landscaping if you buy, appliances and furniture and draperies even if you don't. The chances of your old possessions making a perfect fit are slim, and you'll probably want to decorate a new home in a new way.

Be realistic. Many people have found that the move from a large house to a smaller house has not saved much money in an era of higher interest rates and inflated housing costs. Higher-priced houses, in some areas, are actually more of a bargain these days than more moderate-priced residences. There are fewer of the latter, they are more in demand, and prices are inflated to meet that demand. Maintenance costs, on the other hand, are undeniably higher in a larger and older home. There are other alternatives, of course, rental apartments and condominiums among them, which will be examined in the next chapter.

Was the solidifying of good friendships one of your retirement goals? Then the question of moving or not moving takes on additional significance. If you're starting out on a campaign to make new friends, then it won't matter as much where you are. If you've moved so many times in your working life that you have no roots anywhere, no close friends, you can consider the merits of moving on a purely objective basis. But if you have good close friends, with whom you've shared your life over the years, if moving would take you away from the two or three or five people who mean the most to you, then think carefully. "Human relationships are the most important thing," says Leo Baldwin, housing consultant for the American Association of Retired Persons, "much more important than real estate."

You may have more than one retirement goal. You probably do and, in fact, you should. Make a list of your goals and put them in order of importance. Then you can play a matching game, determining which goals will be met by moving—and which by staying put.

CONSIDER ALL THE ALTERNATIVES

Think about the kind of life-style you want and the kind of person you are. Consider the alternatives in terms of pure physical space. And don't succumb to pressure. If you plan to move, you owe it to yourself to suit yourself. Your former neighbors may be sublimely happy in their city apartment. That doesn't mean that you would be—or that it's the only possibility to consider. Your children may say, with the best intentions in the world, "Golden Acres sounds great. You won't have any worries about security or activities. Why don't you sell your house and buy a unit there?" Golden Acres may indeed be an ideal place to live—but decide for yourself, without succumbing to pressure from your children or from the commercial interests whose profits stem from Golden Acres.

Be sure to evaluate the alternatives for yourself, Leo Baldwin urges, and keep as many options open as possible. Try not to buy on impulse. Surprising numbers of people, conservative people who comparison shop before buying a toaster, buy real estate on the spur of the moment. The decision may be the right one, but doubts may creep in if you make the decision in a hurry or under pressure. Slow down, don't be in a hurry, and consider your to-move-or-not-to-move decision from every angle, subconsciously as well as consciously. If, inside, you really don't want to move, or to move to a particular place, all the rational arguments in the world shouldn't be allowed to make a difference. You will only be unhappy later on.

COMMUNICATE

Perhaps the most important element in successful decision making is communication, bouncing your ideas against the people who matter to you. Decision making is set, usually unconsciously, in the context of comparing notes and goals with another person, a spouse or child or friend. You can, of course, make decisions alone, but it takes a more conscious effort. You must try to see the implications of alternative decisions (am I likely to be lonely if I move? or lonelier here if I'm no longer working and all my neighbors are?), sort out what's important (I'd rather be in a young community, even if my neighbors are working; it's livelier), and see the consequences (if I stay, I'll have to join a club or do some volunteer work to meet some other retirees). When all of this is sorted out, out loud or in your thoughts, a decision can be made.

People who live alone, however, are the only ones who should embark on solo decision making when it comes to moving. People who live with others are looking for long-range trouble if they make major decisions on a unilateral basis. You may move to your Shangri-La, but if your partner is unhappy, your dream can rapidly become a nightmare. And even if your partner accepts the move, what will happen when one of you outlives the other? What will happen in such a circumstance if you both were eager about the move—and what will happen if one of you was not?

Communication involves more than announcing your intentions. It involves shared decision making, in a context where each can express hopes and fears and concerns. It isn't easy. There are always emotional undercurrents. One man, for instance, thought of retirement in terms of taking it easy, and taking it easy in terms of Florida. His wife heard "Florida" and panicked. "Every time he said Florida I got nuts. It's geriatric country down there. I don't want to be buried alive." But, she goes on, "How can I be so selfish? If this is what he really wants, maybe I should go." With these guilt feelings, she never complained openly, but she continued to think of the proposed move in terms of being buried. Fortunately, her concern did surface before a move was made. After talking it through, and making deliberate trade-offs on a one-for-you and one-for-me basis, they reached an agreement: so many months in Florida, so many months back in Pennsylvania, at least on a trial basis. With open communication—and mutual goodwill—they reached a solution.

One way to clarify your own priorities, and to resolve differences of opinion, is to make a planning board of all your options. In this procedure, suggested by Sidney Simon of the University of Massachusetts, you make out a slip of paper for each of your housing choices. The slips should include every possibility, not only housing types ("condominium" or "rental apartment") but location ("Florida" or "the town where I grew up" or "staying right here") and anything meaningful to you ("near the children" or "a college town where I can take classes"). Collect all your slips in an envelope over a period of time, while you are gathering information about your options. Then open the envelopes and review the slips of paper. Place them in order of their importance to you. It sounds simple, but writing out the choices and actually arranging them before you does clarify their relative importance.

If you are married, you and your spouse should each make a set of duplicate slips. When the envelope is opened and the choices read, each places the slips in order of personal importance. A comparison can then be made, and agreement reached. It may be easy: "We kept talking Arizona because everyone we know seems to be moving there, but we found out it was on the bottom of both our lists. We don't want to go to Arizona." And it may be more difficult: "I still want to live near the children and Pete still wants to stay here. I don't know how we'll decide," says Anne. The planning-board process is still worthwhile; once other possibilities are eliminated from consideration, Anne and Pete can devote their attention to their topmost choices. They can list their reasons, positive and negative, for wanting to live where they do. They can compare and discuss those reasons and reach a compromise.

Make your decision after determining your priorities, examining all the alternatives, and communicating with the people in your life. Then if your decision is to stay put, try to look ahead: make any major repairs or necessary purchases before you retire, while an income is still coming in. Make your home as comfortable and as safe as possible. A first-floor bedroom and bath and accessible laundry facilities become increasingly important as the years go by, as do nonskid flooring, adequate lighting, and so on. You might just as well think about it now.

If your decision is to move, your biggest question may be "when." Try, if possible, to detach the move from the retirement itself; there is no particular reason why they should take place together and there are good reasons why they should not. Retirement is a time of transition, of getting used to a new way of life. Why couple it with more transition, with the stress of giving up familiar surroundings and familiar possessions for a new location? Why leave your community and your neighborhood friends at the same time that you leave your job and your business associates? Why not wait and make your decision after retirement, after you see how your new life shapes up in your present home for a year or so? Or if you're determined to move, and you can arrange it, why not move before retirement?

Some people phase into retirement living by moving to their retirement home in advance: a nearby adult community or a smaller house or an apartment. Others buy a weekend or vacation home, with an eye to future full-time living. An early move has an advantage: you can become part of the community. "We had friends, church affiliation, and many contacts with people in the retirement setting before we moved there full-time. . . . In fact, we lived in both places for nine years—so there was no adjustment or disappointment when we retired." It does take time to adjust to a move, to make new friends, and to feel at home, no matter how well planned the move may be. That adjustment process may be easier to take if it occurs either before or after retirement.

Whatever you do, don't move out of impulse. Don't move because other people think it's a good idea. And don't move thinking that life will be totally different. Move, if you do, because you want to. Move after careful consideration. And move remembering, as one wise retiree has said, "you take yourself with you."

7

Where Do
You Want to Live?

If you've decided to move, for whatever well-thought-out reason, you still have decisions to make. Where to? With what kind of financial commitment? What size living unit? In what kind of community?

The alternatives, at least in theory, may seem overwhelming: private ownership or rental or cooperative or condominium, detached house or townhouse or apartment or mobile home, city or suburb or exurbia, in the North or the South or in between. In practice, of course, your choice may be limited: you may not have the money to move where you would like, you may have obligations that limit your mobility, the area you have chosen may not contain the housing you prefer, you may simply have distinct preferences that (mercifully) narrow your choice. A closer look at all the alternatives, however, may open some neglected doors.

Location may be the single most important factor in choosing a home at any time of life. It's no less true at retirement. During your working and family-rearing years you need a home convenient to business, in a location good for raising children. In your retirement years you need an easily maintained home conducive to the life you want to lead, in an area compatible with your life-style.

If your retirement life-style is or will be outward turning, community based, you particularly need to choose the community with care. If your life tends to be inward oriented, centered around activities within the home, the choice of community is still important: people who cherish their privacy are not particularly happy in a community where group activity is the norm. "I like this house," says one such woman, "and the neighborhood is attractive. But I didn't realize how much pressure I would feel. People here just don't understand when I say I don't want to square dance and I don't want to play cards and I don't want to join the social club."

Many people choose a residence itself, attracted by room size or appearance or by a particular desirable feature, with only a cursory glance at location. Yet the house of your dreams in the wrong location will not remain the house of your dreams for long. Pay attention to location, if you are considering a move. Pay attention to region, to community, and to neighborhood. The region, an area with distinct geography and climate, is your first consideration if you plan a long-distance move; the community, the choice among city and suburb and exurbia, comes next; the neighborhood, the specific spot within a community within a region, is last and, perhaps, most important of all.

SELECTING A REGION

Where, given absolutely free choice, would you like to live? Is climate your major concern? In the southern United States you can do a large part of your living outdoors—when it isn't too hot and muggy to bear. You'll have the company of many other retirees in some southern communities, too, which may or may not be to your liking. In the North you can enjoy the changing seasons—and occasionally be trapped by them as well. You may enjoy the company of people of many different ages—and you may feel out of place as a retiree in the world of the working.

What do most retirees prefer? Once again there are myths to dispel. We tend to think of the sun belt as "retirement country." And it's true, 16% of Florida's population is over 65, many of them relatively recent arrivals to the state. Yet fewer than 5% of retirees who move leave their home states; a still smaller fraction moves south. The central states, in fact, states not known for the equanimity of their climate, have the largest concentration of older people. In each of the seven states in the geographical heart of the United States—Arkansas, Iowa, Kansas, Missouri, Nebraska, South Dakota, and Oklahoma—people over 65 make up at least 12% of the population.

In many recent instances, furthermore, retirees who move are choosing to move north. Areas long popular for summer vacations, such as upper Michigan and the mountains of northern California, the Ozarks in Arkansas and the Poconos of Pennsylvania, are increasingly popular for year-round living among retirees who like the winter quiet and the quarterly change of seasons. A note of caution, however: The choice of a summer vacation region often equals the choice of a rural community, with all its advantages and disadvantages. The isolation of the countryside, so much enjoyed when the outdoors beckons, may become dull and depressing in the confinement of winter. The isolation of the countryside, so much enjoyed when you are healthy and active, can become frightening when ill health sets in. Rural regions often don't have too much in the way of medical care; what they do have may be inaccessible.

You may bypass the regional dispute, as so many retirees do, by staying in the region in which you have been living. It may not be perfect, but no place is. It may not be perfect, but you know its shortcomings and have long since adjusted to them. You may decide to move, however, within the region. Perhaps you moved to the suburbs years ago for the sake of the children. They are grown, the house is too big, and the city looks increasingly attractive. Perhaps, on the other hand, you have lived in the city for its convenience to business and now long for a piece of land to call your own.

SELECTING A COMMUNITY

When you look into a new community, be practical. Investigate thoroughly. If you plan a long-distance move, try an extended visit first, if at all possible—not just a vacation in vacation surroundings and climate, but an off-season, several-month-long residence. Rent a place to live, and try to blend with the community. If you can't manage the time before retirement, and you're determined to move, don't burn your bridges: rent out your present dwelling and rent a place to live in the new community. You may find that it's the place of your dreams—and you may find that it is not.

If neither of these alternatives is practical in your circumstances, find out as much as you can at a distance. Write to the Chamber of Commerce, see if the local League of Women Voters has a "Know Your Town" brochure, subscribe to the local newspaper. The local paper is a gold mine of information. It will tell you what organizations are active in the area, what recreational activities are popular, what job opportunities may be available, what the politics are like, what prices to expect for food and clothing and the other necessities of life.

The community you choose, after all—rural or urban or suburban—will have a significant impact on your life-style and on the roles you play. It's hard to be a frequent theatergoer in most rural communities. It's difficult to snowmobile and snorkel in the midst of a large city. You have to decide what activities mean the most, what life-style suits your personality (and, of course, that of your spouse if you are married). Different communities have different attractions.

You may prefer an urban environment: "I thought about moving to the sun belt," says a New York City retiree, "but I don't enjoy card games, Mah-Jongg, or swimming pools, and I'm not a great bingo player. Here I go to a museum a week, lectures, I have a Philharmonic subscription. I don't know if you'd call it a sense of purpose, but in New York I manage to fill my days doing things I enjoy. I suppose I'm living a shiftless life here too—but I don't feel like I am." Or you may prefer a less congested, quieter area: "I don't want to live on top of other people. Here I have my privacy. I have my own garden. I have good neighbors, good but not nosy. And the town provides a lot of things I like, the community greenhouse for instance. I spend a lot of time there, with the Garden Club and on my own. I couldn't do that in a city."

The city, of course, may be too crowded for some, too dirty, too noisy, too crime ridden. The suburbs, and exurbia too, may seem too quiet, too dull—and too isolated. If you don't drive, in most of this country outside metropolitan centers you're out of luck. There are always trade-offs to be made. You may have to accept a degree of isolation in order to have the outdoor sports you particularly want. You may give up the theater for the sake of peace and quiet. You may relinquish a preferred life-style for the accessibility of quality medical care. You may move closer to family and away from friends—or the other way round. No one community can offer everything. But make your trade-offs consciously. In considering any retirement region or community, look at all the significant factors:

- What's the climate like, on a year-round basis? Don't be too quick to give up snow for sun or vice versa without an off-season sample. Consider temperature, rainfall, humidity, active insect life as well.
- How big is the population? Is it the same all year round? What's the age mix?
- Consider the tax structure, and the burden borne by individuals. Consider, again, the age mix of the community: more children need more schools and playgrounds; more schools and playgrounds cost money; the money comes from taxes.
- Consider the services provided by taxes: fire and ambulance

and police protection, hospitals and libraries and museums and recreation facilities. A volunteer fire department may cost you less in property taxes, more in fire insurance. A local museum, whether you visit it or not, may add to the community and hence to the value of your home.

- How accessible are all these services? How accessible are medical and dental care, shopping, and religious and civic organizations?
- Is there a transportation system? what kind? Will you be able to get to all these services and facilities if you can't drive? or don't want to?

SELECTING A NEIGHBORHOOD

Once you've answered all these questions to your satisfaction, once you've selected your region and your community, the neighborhood comes next. In an isolated rural area, where your nearest neighbor is miles away, or in a newly planned community, where the entire development is marked by homogeneity, neighborhood may not exist as such. Anywhere else—in a city, large or small, in a suburb or town—the neighborhood makes a difference. It makes a difference in terms of convenience, in terms of stability, and in terms of character.

You will want to be near shopping, for example, but probably not so near that commercial development encroaches on residences—unless of course, you choose a big-city high rise where convenient shopping is right downstairs. You will want a stable or improving neighborhood, not one in a downward spiral. Look for the existence of zoning codes and a master plan. Look for well-maintained property. Watch out for an abundance of "for sale" signs, or for rental properties in an area of one-family homes. Watch out for rapid turnover and many vacancies in an apartment building or development.

The neighborhood's character, determined by the age and social mix of its residents, will affect you. Evaluate it, and your own preferences, before you move. Do you want a neighborhood full of the lively chatter of small children or the comings and goings of teen-agers? Or will you prefer the quiet of a neighborhood where most residents are at or close to retirement age? Are you stimulated by mixing with people of different backgrounds and occupations? Or do you want a neighborhood where people are much the same, with the same values, goals, and interests? Are you comfortable with the outdoor barbecue set? Or are you more in tune with a golf-club crowd? Perhaps what you really want is to be near a college, with its lectures and concerts and course offerings—and to live near people who care about similar things. There is, of course, no one answer. What one person finds reassuring, another finds dull; what one finds stimulating, another finds discordant. Analyze your own likes and dislikes before you select a retirement home. Then analyze the type of housing you want.

SELECTING A HOME

If you've decided to move because the old family homestead is too big and too difficult to maintain, then you want a smaller easy-to-care-for residence. That definition, however, can be met in several ways: by a smaller, newer detached house, by a townhouse, by an apartment, or by a mobile home. If you've chosen the region, community, and neighborhood you want, your decision will be influenced by the type of housing available in that community. Many communities, especially suburbs with large-lot zoning restrictions, do not have apartments; a great many communities prohibit mobile homes. Such suburbs have largely excluded the young and the elderly, an exclusion which is increasingly under attack. A fight is under way in many suburbs, right now, between older adults who feel the need for apartments (and feel their towns owe them something for years of tax paying) and governing bodies afraid of changing zoning regulations to permit apartments. Change is well overdue and, all too slowly, under way.

If you do have free choice, however, how do you decide?

If you choose a private home, you get space and privacy—plus responsibility for upkeep and repairs. Single-family detached houses, the traditional conventional form of housing in this country, come in all shapes and sizes and conditions. At this stage of your life you will want to minimize maintenance chores, to choose a house in good condition, with interior and exterior finishes that require little care. New houses, however, are expensive. Between 1967 and 1977 the average new single-family home rose in cost from $24,600 to $52,300. Older homes are less expensive, but usually require more attention. Unfortunately, too, in many settled areas the smaller, less expensive homes which might be attractive to older adults are often in less attractive neighborhoods. To find a smaller all-on-one-level house, you may have to move to the outskirts, to newly built-up areas—and you may not want to.

If you are willing to cope with stairs, however, you may find it easier to find the house you want in the neighborhood you want. You may even find what may be the perfect solution: a house with a master bedroom and bath on the first floor and extra rooms upstairs which can be ignored most of the time (closed off, in fact, to save heat) but put to good use when the family visits. You get the most advantageous tax treatment when you sell a home if you buy another, whether a conventional home or a condominium. You also get a break on taxes if you sell when you're over 55. It's worth waiting, if you plan to sell. But you may not want to sell at all. In that case you might consider converting part of your home, if zoning regulations permit, to an income-producing rental unit.

APARTMENTS, COOPERATIVES, CONDOMINIUMS

You can also find all-on-one-level living in an apartment—plus maintenance by others and the freedom (not often found in a house) to lock the door and walk away when you want to travel. Apartments may be found in urban high-rise structures, and in suburban garden apartments and low-rise buildings. They may be in modern elevated buildings, complete with elaborate recreational facilities, or they may be in older walk-up buildings, or in anything in between. They may be rented on a month-to-month basis, or with the security of a lease; they may be owned, either cooper- atively or as a condominium.

In a cooperative, usually a high rise in a large city, you buy a share in the corporation that owns the building, then lease your unit from the corporation; your monthly assessment covers your share, based on apartment size, of the total mortgage, taxes, and maintenance costs for the whole building. You usually must secure approval from the board of directors (who are elected by the residents) when you wish to remodel your unit or to sell.

Condominium ownership, increasingly popular in both apart- ments and townhouse developments, involves individual owner- ship of your residence and joint ownership of common grounds and facilities. Because you buy your own residence, you must arrange your own mortgage and pay your own taxes. You are also responsible for your share of overall operating expenses. Where there are elaborate recreational facilities, operating expenses can be high—and they have been known to rise sharply. Try to find out, before you buy, what you can expect. In a condominium, unlike a cooperative, you have the right to do anything you like with your own unit, including selling it to anyone you please. External renovations, however, may be restricted by the condo- minium association to which all owners must belong.

Either way, owned or rented, apartment living is a special kind of living. It is special in terms of compactness and in terms of neighborliness—or the lack of it. It may take some getting used to, especially if you've spent many years in a house of your own. Some retirees like apartment living very much. "We finally pared down our possessions, got rid of the clutter, and feel as if we're in charge instead of being slaves to a house." Others feel confined, and are unhappy. "Moving to an apartment sounded good, but then I realized none of my furniture would fit. I can't give up all my things. I just can't do it." What's your reaction?

TOWNHOUSES

Townhouse living, increasingly popular, is a compromise in some ways between living in a detached house and living in an apartment. The townhouse usually offers more living space than an apartment. It may actually be an attached house, with two full floors plus basement and garden and garage. And the townhouse owner, whether the unit is a condominium or is owned outright, is often part of an association, which will take care of maintenance should he wish to travel. Townhouse neighbors, on the other hand, are close neighbors—which may or may not suit you. Some people are bothered by neighbors watching their comings and goings; others are reassured when someone cares. Townhouses are usually built in clusters, with houses sharing adjoining walls. Each house has a small private area for landscaping or vegetable gardening or whatever, while other green areas are communally maintained and enjoyed. This townhouse concept makes efficient use of available land, concentrates services, and is thus economically popular with both builders and buyers. Townhouse residences exist in planned communities, including "adult" villages. They are also springing up on the outskirts of traditional suburbs and attracting a mix of ages and family groups.

MOBILE HOMES

Mobile-home living is another increasingly popular option among retired adults. Mobile homes, of course, are not really mobile. But they are efficient and compact, appealing to one- and two-person families. They are also relatively inexpensive: The average price for 14-feet-wide (single-wide) units sold in 1977 was about $13,000; double-wide units, which provide some 1,900 square feet of living space (about three-quarters that of a typical detached house) averaged $18,000. This price does not include set-up costs (concrete pad, supports, steps, et cetera) which will add about 15% to the purchase price. It does not include such optional items as carports and patios. It does not include land; monthly site rentals range from $60 to $150, even more in resort-type parks. But it does include furniture and appliances, which may or may not be to your choice.

Mobile homes can be set up on private property, where zoning regulations permit. Or they can be located in a mobile-home park or community. Such a community should be chosen with care. Many are for adults only. Many are well run, spacious and pleasant, with swimming pools and recreational facilities. Others are shoddy, ill kept, run-down eyesores. The difference is obvious. What may be less obvious is that some parks, nice-looking or not, may be tightly run, so tightly run that residents are hemmed in by arbitrary restrictions. Children may be forbidden one month, permitted the next. Dogs may be prohibited, or allowed at a monthly fee. Overnight guests may be severely limited. Evictions may be totally at the park owner's whim. The only way to find out is to visit the community at different times, in bad weather as well as good, and talk with residents. Find out what the particular community has to offer, and whether residents have any voice in its operations. Find out about rules and regulations, and decide whether you can live with them.

And decide whether mobile-home living, where neighbors are just a few steps away, is for you. It's a close and congenial way of life for those who choose it. "In a conventional house you aren't going to have this selection of friends, you aren't going to have people so close, neighbors that are like you and understand you." But the life is too close, too congenial, for some.

SHARED HOUSING: FRIENDS

If you've ruled out mobile homes and if finances are a problem in your post-retirement living, or if you don't care to live alone, there are two other possibilities: a joint living arrangement with friends, and moving in with children. Shared housing with friends, or with relatives, can work out very successfully. It can also be total disaster. For example, two women who had known each other for years, vacationed together, and enjoyed each other's company retired together to a house in New Hampshire. "They hate each other now," says a relative. "They used to be independent, sharing as they wanted to. Now they're financially locked in, dependent, and bitter. One is sick and needs care; the other resents having to give the care. They're constantly sniping at one another, constantly backbiting. It's a pity. They were the best of friends, and they're ending their years in bitterness."

Careful planning, and evaluation of personalities, is essential if shared housing is to work. If your friend persists in being cheerful at 6 A.M. while you take hours to wake up and face the day, there is a potential for conflict. If one of you is neat and the other messy, chalk up another area of dissension. If one of you is a careful shopper and the other is careless with money, or if one of you has far more retirement income than the other, there can be a problem. All the minor and major irritations that can plague a marriage can be even worse with nonmarried house sharers.

But sharing, carefully considered, can work. An eighty-one-year-old woman who had a successful sharing arrangement for thirteen years before moving to a retirement home points out that:

> two friends—or relatives, for that matter—should be very sure that their needs, tastes, likes, and dislikes are compatible before making more or less permanent arrangements. . . . We talked everything that we could think of as being important—particularly finances—over beforehand. My friend has had a larger income than I. We have shared capital expenditures . . . half and half, but she proposed that for running expenses we set up a joint checking account into which we should put the first of each month an amount proportionate to our incomes—which I accepted. This made it possible for her to enjoy more comforts and luxuries than if

we tailored our budget to conform to the share I could contribute, and to share them with me, as she wished to do, in a sensible, fair, and frictionless way. We each had our own personal checking account for our own personal expenses—everything except for food, electricity, household and yard help, and such household expenses.

SHARED HOUSING: CHILDREN

Moving in with children is something else. While it can be successful (and sometimes, for health or financial reasons, there is no choice), such a move should be carefully considered. Your children may feel they "should" ask you to be with them; you may think you "should" go. But think long and hard before saying yes. Conflicts over behavior and money and habits that can create tension between spouses or friends can create an almost intolerable emotional burden for parents and children. It's hard for you to shed the role of "parent." It's harder still for your children, even in their forties and fifties, to shed the role of "child." Remembered dependency, guilt, and pride all interfere. So if you are considering sharing a residence with your children, be sure to discuss, openly and fully, all the arrangements which will need to be made, physical and financial and emotional:

- Will you have privacy? Will they? You should have a space of your own, preferably not one taken from an unwilling youngster. And you should, in turn, respect the privacy, physical and emotional, of your children and of *their* children. You will want to feel welcome in the family living room—but you will not be there when teen-agers entertain or their parents need a quiet hour together.
- Will you maintain your own social life and activities? Will they? If you have to leave your own friends far behind in order to join your children, try to make new friends. Join a club or an organization, but don't be dependent upon your children for all your activities and companionship. You each need to lead your own lives.

- Can you maintain an emotional distance? Can you refrain from interfering—and from silently registering disapproval? Don't take sides in a dispute between your child and his or her spouse. Don't interject your opinion when their children are being disciplined. You may never have given your son the use of the car when he was a teen-ager—but that fact will not interest either your son or his teen-ager.

- Will you be allowed to do your share in the running of the household? You will want to participate, to do what you can, both for the sake of your own ego and for the sake of the family. You are likely to feel totally useless if you become a permanent guest. You will not, on the other hand, want to be taken advantage of, and it may be best to lay out the ground rules in advance: how much baby-sitting are you willing to do? how much housework? How much do you think is fair? And what do your children think?

- What financial arrangements will be made? If you can afford to contribute to the running of the joint household, you will feel better if you do so. If your money is the only way in which your children can buy a house, however, you may want to think twice. If you supply the down payment, for instance, and they agree to handle the month-to-month operating expenses, what happens if their circumstances change? or if they must relocate for business reasons? Will you be left holding the bag? It's very difficult to be objective about money with your own children, but it is very important to do so—for both your sakes.

Don't expect the adjustment to be easy if you move in with your children; both you and your offspring will have to adapt, to compromise. But if you can arrange all these elements to everyone's satisfaction, and if you can all remain flexible, living together may work out well. You will have the chance to keep in touch with younger people and their concerns (can you discuss child-rearing or business practices without always bringing up the past?); you will have the opportunity to really know your grandchildren (when they're noisy and troublesome, as well as when they're on best behavior); you can share the warmth (and the occasional inevitable conflicts) of an extended family.

RETIREMENT COMMUNITIES

The flip side of the living-with-children coin, with all its advantages and disadvantages, may be the all-of-one-age community, with all *its* advantages and disadvantages. Residential segregation by age is not uncommon. It exists in new suburban developments of three- and four-bedroom split-levels, in older towns with large-lot zoning and hard-to-pay property taxes, in high-rise apartments along the Miami Beach "Gold Coast." It also exists, by deliberate design, in the "for adults only" communities springing up around the nation.

Are planned adult communities a good thing? Some, of course, say yes: "You can always find companionship here," says one retiree. "All you have to do is walk down to the clubhouse and see what's going on. Back home, nothing was going on. Most people were at work during the day." "I like all the activities," says another, an ex–power plant supervisor who chose a retirement village twenty-five miles from his former home (85% of retirement-village residents in one major study came from the same region). "You could sit and vegetate if you didn't move somewhere like this, and I didn't want to vegetate." Yet others, many others, say no. Only 23% of the people over 65 queried in the 1974 Harris poll said that they prefer to spend most of their time with people their own age, while 74% preferred the company of people of all different ages. Or as one sixty-nine-year-old puts it: "Don't 'hole up' in a 'senior citizen' enclave or retirement home until you must. Stay where you can get mad at the school kids cutting across your lawn."

Getting mad at school kids may be one way to keep the juices flowing, but it's certainly not everyone's choice. Many older adults prefer peace and quiet. Reactions to retirement communities as such, positive or negative, tend to be intense, however. A scholarly observer, Gordon L. Bultena of the University of Wisconsin, notes that retirement communities can be viewed as a new concept in meeting the needs of the elderly—or as an unnatural and stultifying environment. Retirement-community residents are pictured as people who can remain physically and socially active, avoiding the isolation and loneliness of more conventional surroundings—or as "bored and disillusioned persons who lead shallow lives dominated by a hedonistic pursuit of happiness." Among older persons themselves, reactions are equally extreme. At one end of the scale: "I love it here. I wish I'd gotten older sooner!" and "I'm talking all my friends into coming here" (most customers, according to developers, are referrals from satisfied residents). At the other end, there is total horror: "A retirement village? God forbid!"

Objectively speaking, insofar as it is possible to be objective, what are the pros and cons of an adult community? On the plus side, and at the top of most lists, is the relative low cost and high level of amenities, the basic fact that the purchase is "a lot for the money." Another factor, foremost in the minds of many older adults, is security. Many retirement communities advertise a guarded gatehouse, where visitors are screened; most have security patrols. Some villages, in built-up areas, are enclosed by fences. Others, in rural surroundings, are wide open but isolated. Another plus is characteristic of any condominium or apartment or residential-association development, whether age segregated or not: ease of maintenance and freedom to travel, without the cares of home ownership. Another plus, a very important one to most people who choose an adult community, is a wide selection of activities and the availability of people to join in. Most planned villages center around a clubhouse, where offerings include card rooms and socials, crafts and hobby groups, classes and lectures and amateur theatricals. Many also have swimming pools, golf courses, and other recreational amenities. The presence of all these facilities, plus the presence of a large leisure class of retired people (and potential pool of friends), sets the scene for an easy way of life. It's easier to adjust to retirement, some say, when everyone around you is doing the same.

But all is not roses in the retirement-village garden. Most of the plus factors can also, depending on your personal perspective, be viewed as minuses. People seeking "a good buy" are not necessarily seeking isolation—but isolation does exist. "Why go outside? everything I want is here." Security patrols and guarded gates may keep intruders out—but some see them as keeping residents in, at least psychologically, and isolated from the community at large. "It's like a reform school," one visitor commented. "You can't go in or out without identification." Security, furthermore, has more than one meaning. "That an aging population of white middle-class property owners, many of them in poor health," Jerry Jacobs writes in a scholarly but caustic study of one "typical" retirement village, "seek 'security' in an isolated social environment which has no police department, no fire department, or major health facilities, is an enigma."

The association may provide carefree living, but it also provides rules and regulations that make the community run smoothly—but which some people see as unpleasant regimentation. Must all exterior trim be the same? Must all visits by grandchildren be restricted in length? The activity program fills the time—but says one not-altogether-happy resident, "Everyone does the same things all the time. Everyone says the same things all the time. It's dull as hell." The presence of all-alike people, retirees who relish their leisure and their leisure activities, is comforting to some—and stultifying and boring to others, to people who prefer the stimulation of cross-age contacts. "Sure, we're old," says a woman in her mid-seventies who tried retirement-community living and didn't like it, "but when you live around just other old people, pretty soon you start to feel older yourself. I prefer living where there are people of every age. You keep up with things and don't feel like you crawled off in some corner to die."

The heart of the argument, of course, is this question of age segregation. It's age segregation that provides the pool of friends with time on their hands. It's age segregation that feeds the leisure-oriented life-style. And it's life-style itself that you must evaluate, if you are considering a retirement community. "The home itself is secondary; the home can be changed," says Terry Bickel, vice-president–sales for Leisure Technology, Inc., a major developer of adult communities. "The most important thing is the life-style and whether or not you will fit into it. Talk to residents, not just to salespeople, talk to friends who've moved previously, before you decide to buy."

You should, in fact, evaluate an adult community as carefully as you would evaluate any community. They are not all the same. Far from it. Some are massive, with thousands of units; others are small. Some are condominium units, with maintenance provided; some are individually owned, where maintenance is a do-it-yourself proposition. Some are high-rise developments; some are townhouse clusters. Some cost less than conventional housing; others cost far more. Some provide transportation; some do not. Some appeal to poker players; others draw the country-club crowd. Some have constantly scheduled activities, with a full-time recreation director ("We're a summer camp for old folks, and I'm the camp director"). Others just have a clubhouse, waiting to be used—or not. One new community in New Jersey, characterized by its developers as midway between overscheduled and non-scheduled, listed 1,500 events in its community calendar for 1977.

Some retirement communities have residents with an average age of seventy-three. Others cater to people in their fifties. Newer developments, where the minimum age at entry is fifty-two or fifty-five (even forty-eight in some instances, where sales needed a boost), have a younger population. Many of the initial purchasers are still employed. As these initial residents age, however, the average age in the development will also rise. If you are in your fifties when you move in, you will be dealing with two genera-tions—your own and the next older generation (there's at least one instance, in fact, of parents and children buying separate homes in the same retirement community). As you age, so will your neighbors and, despite some turnover, you will find yourself among older and older people. This is when some find retirement communities most depressing. "Everyone's sick," it's been said, "and the ambulance siren is such a constant background noise that it's almost possible (almost, not quite) to tune it out."

It's impossible to generalize, of course: retirement communities are an ideal haven for some people, the worst place in the world for others. You must evaluate any possible move, whether to a retirement community or anywhere else, in terms of both practical matters (how much will it cost? will the move bring you closer to family and friends? or farther away?) and in terms of your own life-style and personality (do you like organized activities? do you want to be with people of similar age and interests? Will you thrive on intellectual stimulation—and be miserable without it?). Try to find out, insofar as possible, what you're getting into— before you make a commitment.

Look ahead, too. The first post-retirement move is not necessarily the last. Consider: Will this community meet your needs, suit your life-style, when you are older still? Will the place that's right for your sixties be equally right for your seventies and eighties? Will this community, this way of life, be comfortable for the surviving spouse of a close-knit couple? or is it a community built around couples? a place too far from "home"? You may not be able to answer these questions now, but at least consider the issues they raise. And make your move, if you make one, as thoughtfully as you can.

Human Options

8

Two by Two

Diane and Rob D. call their retirement years a "second honey-moon," even better than the first. "We always enjoyed each other's company," says Diane, "but we never had enough time. Too many other things interfered. Now that we've both retired, we're busier than we ever thought possible. We do things together, but we spend lots of time just talking, too, getting reacquainted. We have so much to say!"

The P. marriage, on the other hand, after holding together through thirty-eight years, disintegrated with the togetherness of retirement. "Bicker, bicker, bicker," Marian said to her lawyer as she filed for divorce. "We got along fine until Al retired. Then he had nothing to do but bother me. Day in, day out, he stood over me and criticized; I couldn't even wash the dishes right. I tried kidding him out of it. Then I tried talking to him seriously, telling him to get out of the house, find something to do. Nothing helped. I can't take it anymore."

Arlene L. might prefer someone telling her how to wash the dishes: she retired at fifty-nine, so that she and Dick could enjoy his retirement, traveling as they'd planned for years, but Dick died before realizing their long-held dream to see the Far East. Arlene was left alone. She's beginning to see old friends again, and to make new ones, but it isn't easy.

If you are married as you move toward your sixties, you have a companion with whom to face the challenges of retirement. You have a relationship which, with attention, will grow and flourish. But you may be in for some surprises, as you and your spouse spend more and more time together, and your relationship undergoes some changes.

No relationship is ever static. There are changes throughout marriage, as circumstances change and as you react to circumstances. There are ups and downs in feelings about each other, at different stages of married life, as well as shifts in the balance of power. Honeymooners, in the first flush of joyful togetherness, often share in making virtually all decisions as well as in performing most household tasks. "We couldn't bear to be parted—and I wouldn't buy so much as a pair of shoes alone." Young couples, as the glow fades a bit, continue to share, although responsibility begins to be divided in the interests of efficiency. Then, through the years, paths often diverge. As the husband becomes increasingly preoccupied with work and the wife with either her own job or children and home, or with both, they often go their own way, to greater or lesser extent. If either changes course in midstream, with a man making a midlife career change or a woman perhaps seeking a career for the first time, the spouse may fail to understand why—or to appreciate the disruptions brought by the change.

Either way, in the course of time, less time is spent together, fewer decisions made jointly. Even in good marriages, husband and wife spend relatively little time together, know little about the way the other spends the day, and may know little about the other's thoughts and feelings. As a result, says Dr. Bernard A. Stotsky, psychiatrist at the University of Washington Medical School, "many couples reach old age without knowing each other very well." With retirement, with long-sought time to spend together, husband and wife too often face each other as strangers.

This may be one reason for late-in-life divorces. How can you live with a stranger when you can't run away from the relationship by going to work each morning? How, too, can you live with a stranger when you're dependent on that stranger and not sure of your own identity? Phoebe Bailey, eastern regional coordinator of Action for Independent Maturity, suggests that some late-life divorces arise from just this situation: "A lot of women between fifty and sixty-five are beginning to wish they'd been born later. Women in this generation are either not working, not independent, or, if they're working, the job is not particularly challenging. Some are frustrated, as a result, and their husbands are threatened by their unhappiness."

Significant numbers of older couples, however, despite gloomy comments about late-life unhappiness, find that freedom from earlier responsibilities and the opportunities to spend more time doing things they like to do gives them a greater appreciation for one another. Retirement, in fact, often strengthens the bond between husband and wife. But retirement does alter the ground rules, and you must get to know each other all over again.

TIME TO BECOME REACQUAINTED

How well do you know your spouse? Do you know what she eats for lunch—or what he wishes for in retirement? Does your spouse know these things, little and big, about you? Have you talked about them? Or do you guess? At a Baltimore company's pre-retirement seminar a husband remarked that he was planning to retire to a house the couple owned in Vermont. To his confusion, his wife burst out, "I'm not going to live *there* in the winter." He was taken aback because they owned the house, after all, and what was more logical than to live there in retirement? But he had failed to discuss the logic with his wife, or even to broach the subject.

What about you? When was the last time you had a serious conversation? discussed your hopes and fears and goals for the future? Now, right now, is the time to strengthen your relationship. Start by assessing where you are. Do you:

- like to do most things together?
- prefer being alone?
- have similar tastes in entertainment and food and friends?
- respect each other's need for privacy?
- make most spending decisions together?
- argue about money?
- find your spouse's habits irritating?
- appreciate your spouse's sense of humor?
- criticize your spouse in public?
- resent being criticized?
- wish your spouse showed more affection?
- frequently lose your temper with your spouse?
- often interrupt each other?
- find certain topics hard to discuss?
- wish your spouse confided in you more?
- tell your spouse about your dreams?
- share your thoughts about books and movies and television?
- ever talk about anything but the house . . . and the children . . . and relatives?

Analyzing your own responses, and comparing them with your spouse, may prove interesting—especially if you learn something new. "We had sort of a vague feeling that we'd grown apart, but hadn't really put our finger on it," one man indicated. "Then we saw how our conversations had changed. When we first got married we could spend hours talking about ourselves, about what we thought and wanted about our philosophies, about our dreams for the future. Then we got involved. We not only got busy with our jobs and our children, we ran out of time and energy to talk about anything else. We'd both come home tired from work and there'd be a problem with the kids or with the plumbing. We haven't even argued about a movie in years . . . and that's the first thing we're going to correct."

Making corrections in a sound marriage gone stale does not require major surgery. Spending time together—going to a movie and arguing about its meaning—is a step in the right direction. So is making yourself aware of your own behavior. Think about it: can you list five things that you have repeatedly asked or scolded or nagged your spouse to do? things that have never been done? How about things your spouse is after you to do—and which you can not or do not wish to do? These things don't count, you say; every marriage is full of little disagreements; your spouse knows you love her/him, even when you nag. Well, *do* you love your spouse? If you do, list five examples of your loving behavior toward your spouse in the last month, five little instances of care and concern and helpfulness. How do the instances of loving behavior measure up against the naggings and scoldings and generally hateful behavior?

It's an old story. We tell people (especially those we are close to) what bothers us and not, too often, what pleases us. Children get the message that parents care only about messy rooms; spouses hear about money shortages or household repairs left undone. We accentuate the negative, not the positive. "I love it when Art takes over dinner. I don't have to cook, and the meal is always interesting—not necessarily good, but interesting, because he's a great experimenter. I always stick to recipes. But why do I always wind up talking about the condition of the kitchen when he's done?"

Sometimes it's hard to say, "Gee, I appreciate your making dinner." Sometimes it's even hard to say, just like that, "I love you." Do you love your spouse? How do you show that you do? By saying "I love you," without being prompted? By a touch or a pat or a look in your eyes? By a perfunctory good-bye and hello kiss at either end of the day? By doing what's expected of you in providing and maintaining the home? There are usually lots of loving words and gestures at the beginning of marriage, when love is new and wonderful, and fewer as the years go by, as love is accepted without thought or comment.

If this is the case in your marriage, if love remains unspoken and minor annoyances build up to obscure the good things you once saw in each other, try what Sidney Simon of the University of Massachusetts calls a "validation" exercise: Sit down with your spouse and, for two minutes by the kitchen timer, tell him what you appreciate about him. They can be little things or big—being on time for appointments or being a good provider or having a good sense of humor, or anything at all. For the next two minutes, have him tell you what he appreciates most about you. No wisecracks, now, this is for real. Then, spend two minutes on self-validation: tell your spouse what you like about yourself and would like him to know and appreciate. The last two minutes, again, is reversed, with your spouse speaking in self-validation. At the end, says Dr. Simon, "spend a minute or so doing a very gentle thing, ping-pong back and forth with what you liked to hear or would like to hear: 'Hey, next time, will you tell me again . . .' or 'Hey, next time, tell me please, that you . . .' " This may seem silly, at first, or even scary, but it's a good way to remind yourself what you like about your spouse—and about yourself. It's a good exercise to repeat, at different times, with different insight.

Most people—some 80% of men, almost 40% of women—are married as they approach retirement. Many have good marriages—and they are fortunate, because people with close family ties adjust more successfully to retirement. But people with good marriages can still benefit from validation. Many, no doubt, have become involved, tired, and uncommunicative at some point over the years. Many simply fall in a rut, take each other for granted. People who are bored with each other can also benefit from validation, from reminding themselves what they once saw in each other. A marriage may seem dull and lifeless, but this is not the time to give up. On the contrary—with just a little effort, well worth expending, marriage in the retirement years can (and should) be better than ever.

Satisfaction levels over the marital life cycle have actually been charted—and satisfaction is highest, according to Harold Feldman of Cornell University, at the beginning of marriage and at the end. In the post-parental years, those lovely twosome years after children have flown the coop, taking with them all the conflicts and worries about their upbringing, married couples are happier than ever. Being together is more fun. So is sex. "We've got privacy and freedom at last. We can go when we please, and stay in when we please. We can even make love in the middle of the afternoon. I don't miss the kids a bit!" Or as Dr. Feldman puts it: "This period, when children are no longer at home, has been described as the 'empty nest' period. I'm not an ornithologist, but it's my understanding that when the nest is empty and the young birds have left, so have their parents." The older generation has "flown off to new adventures."

The post-parental years are a time for your new adventures, for spending time together and doing things together, little things like taking a walk or going out for lunch or browsing in a shop, without having to tell anyone where you're going and when you'll be back—and without having to *be* back at any given time. These are years to enjoy each other's company and to enjoy, if you so desire, a sex life uninhibited by either the fear of pregnancy or children in the house. Sexual activity, it is now known and finally admitted, can continue to the very end of life. All it takes is a willing partner. This postparental period, however, usually begins well before retirement, when many husbands and wives are in their early fifties, with freedom tempered by the continued need to work and to build retirement funds. In a way, these years are a decompression chamber, a halfway step between the responsibilities of parenthood and career building and the total freedom of retirement. With retirement itself, with no schedules and few commitments, you will spend even more time together. Will you enjoy it?

PLAN TO ENJOY

Your marriage may be a good one. You may enjoy each other's company. But you may enjoy that company during evenings, weekends, and once-a-year vacations. Even vacations, with bad luck, can be a problem. Have you ever spent a weekend, intended for golf, confined to a motel room by incessant rain? What did you talk about? How long before you bolted for home? How will you approach twenty-four-hours-a-day, seven-days-a-week togetherness? At home, without the diversions of vacation? Have you thought about how much of that time you will actually spend together? Have you discussed it? Have you thought about what you will actually do with your time? Have you made plans to do so? Have you shared those plans with your spouse?

People often fail to make plans until confronted with the reality of retirement. Things may work out well anyway—"We found plenty to do"—or they may not. "We didn't have a plan," one woman wrote to *Retirement Living* magazine, "and we soon became restless. I became irritable trying to suggest things he might do, and he became oversensitive about being in my way. Finally, we both recognized what we needed was a schedule and routine we both could follow." Their schedule: breakfast out, together, each weekday morning, and afternoons spent separately, pursuing individual interests, with no interruptions permitted. Another couple tried another plan: once a week, they decided, would be "husband's day," a day on which he had to plan what they would do. "It's always a surprise, whatever it is," Audrey says. "Sometimes we poke around a garden shop, sometimes we have a nice lunch out, sometimes Greg dreams up a project at home—like the afternoon we spent weeding out the books in the attic. Whatever, it's a day that's out of my hands—and I like that."

Neither of these plans may be right for you. But it's worth thinking about, worth making some plan that allows for both individuality and togetherness. Look ahead. Picture a week of retirement. Do you like the picture you see? If not, now is the time to take a brush and change the picture. Look at yourselves today. Do you pursue individual interests as well as interests in common? spend leisure time apart as well as together? You should—even the most compatible of couples cannot do everything, endlessly, together. If you try, there will be nothing to talk about, to describe, to share.

Do you have any interests in common? Some marriages survive for years on mutual busyness. "Unfortunately," says one retiree, "since we have absolutely no interests in common, retirement brings far more strain between us than was present when we were both employed." If this is the case in your household, it is long past time to develop some interests in common. Go back to the roots of your relationship, find what brought you together, and build upon it. Look at current enthusiasms and build upon them. "We decided to take folk-dance classes," one man says, "after my wife convinced me to give it a try. We get mental exercise out of learning the routines as well as physical exercise out of doing them. And we've met lots of nice people, of all ages. When we travel, now, we look for folk-dance clubs, and we're always welcomed."

THERE CAN BE PROBLEMS . . .

When no plans are made in advance, no interests developed, it may be difficult to look forward to retirement. But whether or not men look ahead with anticipation, their wives often dread the prospect. "I just know he's going to be under foot all day," say women who do not work outside the home. "He's going to be bored if I go to work and leave him at home," say women who do. Too often where men have not planned ahead, their wives are right. "I can always tell when one of my patients has a recently

retired husband—when she doesn't understand the problem herself," says an internist in Long Beach, California. "She's tense and
nervous, and no wonder. It's always 'Is it time for lunch yet?' and
'Isn't it dinnertime yet?' And the man tracking through the house
constantly, from garden or workshop or garage. . . ."

It's this constant togetherness, a grating get-on-the-nerves
togetherness, made worse by idleness, that ruins retirement for
many couples—at least until they reach an accommodation about
how they will live in this new stage of life. "It's been the worst six
months of my life," one woman wept to a friend. "You never saw
such togetherness. He won't let me out of his sight. When I left for
the store he wanted to know where I was going. Then how long I'd
be gone. And as I backed the car out of the drive he was looking at his
watch, actually checking my departure time!" It's the little things
that can drive a wife to distraction: having to explain who's on the
phone, making lunch each and every day. It's the little things that
perplex a husband: So this is what she does with her time.

Retired men with no other occupation, interests, or activities
can drive their wives crazy, especially if they don't lift a finger to
help around the house. The intention may be good—"I don't want
to take over her job"—but the result is not. Such husbands, around
the house and under foot, make more work for their wives—and
their wives might like to retire too. And retired men who do help
around the house can also drive their wives crazy—if they find
better ways to do everything and don't hesitate to say so. "For
weeks now," Marie Sorenson writes in her tongue-in-cheek but
all-too-true book, *Move Over, Mama,* "Herman has been literally
grabbing things out of my hands, invariably with the same
statement, 'Here, let me show you how to do that.' I mean I have
had to stand like a dumbbell while Herman has shown me a better
way to peel a hard-boiled egg, wash a glass, hold a paring knife,
clean the sink and on and on with lectures about dozens of little
chores I've been doing very well for forty years."

It's silly, you say, to make a fuss about housework. True. But
housework can become the focus of a lot of post-retirement

arguments—if it's allowed to do so. Retired couples should try to get household chores quickly out of the way so that they can go on to other things. It doesn't matter who does what as long as you agree. But you will be happier when you cooperate, says sociologist Gordon Streib, than if you are competitive about who does what—and much happier than when a wife jealously guards her turf against her husband's invasion. When married couples can come to terms with the husband's retirement and restructure the relationship accordingly, they will also be happier. This does not happen when a husband, trying to be helpful, says, "Just pretend I'm not here, honey. Just pretend I'm at work."

A lot depends on the underlying structure of the marriage. Long-lasting marriages tend to be both egalitarian and companionable; the partners regard themselves as equals and/or friends. Even so, there are differences in the balance of power. In some marriages the husband is indisputably in charge. In others the wife rules the roost. But changes do occur over the years. Working women, for example, often wield considerably more power than their nonworking counterparts. Where a woman has always worked outside the home, as in more and more of today's young marriages, the couple have accommodated themselves to this sharing of power. Where an older woman returns to work later in life, however, after years of being a very junior partner in the marriage, the shifting power base may be hard for her husband to take—and for the marriage itself, without a good deal of goodwill, to survive. If the wife's working and assumption of power coincides with the husband's retirement and giving up of power, there may be real problems—unless both partners come to terms with their feelings.

RETIRE TOGETHER?

No matter how long a wife has been working outside the home, however, if she is younger (or older) than her husband, there's a major question to be faced: Should they synchronize retirement?

Should one spouse take early retirement in order to share retirement with the other? "We've been looking forward for years to the day when we could travel without worrying about vacation schedules; we want to take a freighter, without thinking about what day or week we'll return, and see where we wind up. How can we do that if I retire and Nell keeps on working?" Nell, however, is not sure what she wants to do: "Yes, we've planned on traveling, and I'm sorely tempted. But I didn't go back to work until our girls were all in school and it took me a long time to move ahead. Now I'm doing really interesting work, and I'm not sure I'm ready to retire."

The question isn't simple; neither are the alternative solutions. If George retires and Nell keeps right on working, they will have to defer their travel plans. He's sixty-five now, healthy and active, and eager to go. Will he be as eager in five years? If Nell keeps on working, however, the family income—and savings toward travel—will be greater. If she keeps on working until she is eligible for company pension and Social Security, moreover, their post-retirement income will also be greater. Meanwhile, what will George do while Nell is working? He has always helped with the housework, taking on more chores as Nell worked longer hours. But he doesn't really want to be a househusband, just because he's at home and she is not; this is a role reversal for which few men are prepared. He may, however, enjoy a decompression period at home, alone. Some men are just plain happy to be at home, poking about, doing what they want to do, with no one requesting an explanation. "Men don't always want to say who's on the phone either," as Phoebe Bailey puts it. "They may want to feel like kings in their own homes, at least for a while."

But George, eager to travel, may urge Nell to retire. If she does, eager to travel herself as well as to please George, how will it work out in the long run? The freighter trip may be fun but, when it is over, what will take the place of the job she loved? Will she and George make a satisfactory new life or will she be left with a sense of frustration at her incomplete career? If Nell is widowed before she herself has reached retirement age, as is, unfortunately, quite possible, will her grief be worse because she has lost not only George but her own job, on-the-job friends, and income as well? Or will she be sorrier if she kept on working, and they never had the trip they planned?

There are no "right" answers to such questions. Each couple must make its own decision. But whether you decide to retire together or not and whether, in fact, you are both working or not, don't be surprised by changes in your relationship. Retirement brings changes. So does the passage of time. The sex roles inculcated by our society—men are independent, unemotional, and brave; women are dependent, sentimental, and timid—tend to blur with the years. Men become more sensitive in later life, more tuned in to feelings. One sign of this change is that family and friends become increasingly important with the years. Women, at the same time, become more independent and assertive. They stop being "Debbie's mother" and "the department head's wife," and become, at last, their own persons. Or as one indomitable eighty-year-old puts it: "The biggest advantage of living this long is that I don't have to give a damn what anyone thinks. I can do just what pleases me."

Within marriage, however, pleasing "me" is not all there is. If marriage is to work, if it is to continue to sustain you through the retirement years, it takes pleasing each other. It takes planning, together, for the use of increased leisure time. And it takes, above all, good communication.

TALK TO EACH OTHER

In his studies of marriage, conducted over many years, Harold Feldman has found that the more time husbands and wives spend talking to each other, the more likely they are to report a high level of marital satisfaction. The kind of talking that counts, however, is real communication, not talking at but talking with, not just talking but listening as well. A lot of people don't listen. Even when they do, or think they do, understanding is often clouded by their own perceptions—and misperceptions. Husbands and wives, for example, each claim that conversations with each other are more often about subjects of interest to the other.

True communication is important throughout marriage but even more important when it comes to planning for retirement; couples can get along without sharing thoughts and feelings in the commotion of a child-filled house, but when they face each other, and only each other, over the question of what to do and where to live in retirement, they had better communicate. Some couples never did know how to communicate; others forget how. Either way, the consequences can be unpleasant. One couple was about to move to a retirement community; they had put $4,000 down on a home in the new community and had put their house up for sale. Three weeks before moving day, in the midst of preparations, she backed out. He, needless to say, was furious. How could she do this? They'd agreed, hadn't they? But, says the counselor they finally consulted in an effort to resolve their differences and save their marriage, "There had to be signs all along, all along the way, that were being ignored. He is a high-pressure guy who steamrolls over objections, who often doesn't even hear them. She never agreed to the decision at all. He wasn't listening."

Don't fall into this trap. Right now, as you approach retirement, polish your communication skills. All it takes is practice.

Start by listening, by really hearing what your partner has to say. You've probably overheard a conversation, or taken part in one, where each person went on talking without responding to the other, conducting two monologues instead of a dialogue. Where one person, like our steamroller friend above, is so intent on his own purposes that he fails to hear his partner's objections, there is no communication. Where two people are so eager to spill out their own ideas that they do not pause to hear the other, there is no communication either.

Listening isn't always easy. It includes paying attention, physically paying attention. How annoyed do you get when you try to tell your husband something while he has one eye on the television screen? What about when your wife keeps right on balancing the checkbook while you try to tell her about your day? There are times, of course, when talking and doing something else is reasonable. There are other times when undivided attention really matters.

To listen effectively, you must temporarily turn off your own thoughts. Don't spend the minutes while your partner is talking thinking about what you are going to say next. Try to respond to what he is actually saying instead. If you find this difficult, try this technique: Summarize what the other person has said before making your next point, and ask him to do the same for you. It's artificial and it slows down conversation, but it reinforces the habit of listening. It also makes sure you are receiving the message that was delivered instead of a distorted, self-perceived version. If things get really bad, try switching sides in the midst of a disagreement. If you can't assume your partner's arguments, you haven't been listening to them.

Communication includes the whole context in which an interchange takes place—what is said and whether attention is being paid, plus facial expressions and gestures by both speaker and listener. Raised eyebrows are meaningful. Tone of voice is revealing. "I don't believe you" is a single phrase that can sound accusatory or incredulous or distrustful or jocular, depending on the context.

Communication includes speech itself. Do you make yourself clear? Or do you play guessing games? Do you assume that your spouse knows you well enough to know what you mean, what you think, and how you feel? Do you assume that your spouse knows where you're thinking of living, for example, if you've never quite said anything about it? Do you assume that you know what your spouse means to say, or is thinking about a particular issue, or do you hear him out? Unless you are both mind readers, gifted with extrasensory perception, learn to communicate, not guess. If you want something from somebody, whether something tangible (why don't we go to the movies on Sunday?) or intangible (I'm feeling blue, can you comfort me?), say so. Don't set yourself up to be hurt because your spouse "never understands."

Use words that open up communication, too, not words that close it off. Listen to yourself. How often do you use phrases like "You always . . ." or "You should . . ." or "I can't remember the last time you . . ."? Such phrases are verbal triggers, setting off a chain reaction of closed communication and angry feelings. "How can we discuss anything calmly when you always get angry?" is not a question designed to calm the anger; no accusatory statement is. The frustrated spouse could try, instead, what psychologists call "I-messages." Instead of defining the other person's behavior, describe your own feelings: "I'm very upset because we can't seem to discuss this calmly" or "I feel very badly when we disagree; can we reach a compromise?"

It isn't easy, always, to express feelings, even with a spouse. We take so much for granted; "Of course I love you" is too often a response to a request for reassurance. The Marriage Enrichment movement, however, is helping many married couples come to terms with their own feelings and understand their partners; you can adapt the movement's techniques. In Enrichment weekends couples of all ages—from those married a month to those married for forty-five years or more—learn the technique of dialogue, the technique of sharing feelings with one another in a noncritical, nonjudgmental way. When you dialogue, you conduct a "ten and ten," ten minutes of individual written reflection on a given topic and ten minutes of dialogue about the topic, after reading each other's reflections. The dialogue is a quest for understanding, not an opportunity for rebuttal. It concerns feelings, not thoughts. The topic can be almost anything you choose, from simple events in ordinary life to philosophical issues. For example, how do I feel:

• when you bring me a present?
• when the children come to visit?
• when you interrupt something I'm saying?

- when we spend a quiet evening together?
- about getting older?

There's something about putting thoughts in writing, free from facial expressions, body language, and interruptions, that encourages free-flowing feelings. There's something about sharing those feelings, in a time slot limited to ten minutes, and in an atmosphere free of recrimination, that encourages open communication in other times and places.

MAKING DECISIONS

Decision making is enhanced by open communication. Many many decisions are made throughout a married couple's life together, from decisions about what color to paint the bathroom to decisions about where to live and where to send the children to school to decisions about what to do in retirement. At the very beginning, most decisions are made together. Then, over the busy in-between years, each partner usually carves out an independent area for decision making. There's an old joke about that: "My wife makes all the unimportant decisions, and I make the important ones. She decides where we'll live and what kind of job I should have; I decide whether the president is doing the right thing." In actual fact, however, most men (subject, of course, to wide individual differences) make decisions about career and family financial affairs and where the family will live. Most women make decisions about decorating the house and clothing the children. In-between areas are jointly decided. How those joint decisions are reached reveals a good deal about the power structure within the family—and about the state of communication.

Decisions can be reached by consensus, by mutual agreement. Or if there is no consensus, decisions can be reached by accommodation, by compromise, or by concession. When partners accommodate, they agree to disagree, to go their separate ways on a particular issue. When they compromise, they meet each other halfway or, sometimes, they agree on alternating mutually acceptable solutions: this year we go to the lake, next year to the ocean, and that way we're both happy. When people make concessions, one gives way to the other; sometimes right is clearly on one side, sometimes one person is stronger than the other, sometimes a flip of a coin decides who wins.

There are decision-making techniques which can help, however, when you find yourselves at an impasse. First, and most important, put forth all the possible solutions to a particular problem before evaluating any one of them. Brainstorm: throw out ideas without regard to whether or not they are sensible, just to get as many ideas on the table as you possibly can. In brainstorming, tossing ideas into a verbal stew, one idea leads to another, and you may well find yourselves with a realistic solution that would never have occurred to you at all. Don't get bogged down in deciding whether or not you want to move to Florida, in other words, before having a verbal free-for-all of other possibilities. Don't hold back; toss your ideas out and write them down so that you have as long a list as possible. Listen to each other's suggestions with respect; don't rule out anything at this stage, no matter how preposterous it may seem.

Then, and only then, evaluate the list. Put the items on the list, each of you, in order of your preferences; drop the ones you both agree to drop. Then measure the remaining alternatives in terms of their pluses and minuses—and in terms of what is important to you, to you individually and to you jointly. Look at the consequences of each decision: what would actually happen if you did thus and so? Would you be comfortable with that result?

If you're still having trouble reaching a decision, take each other's part, as you did in honing your listening skills. Put forth your husband's reasons for moving to Florida; argue your wife's position for living near the children. You may change your mind, and you may not, but you will begin to understand your spouse's feelings and, in understanding them, be better able to find common ground. If brainstorming worked, in any case, you probably have a third alternative: "Hey, we can't stay in this big house anymore, but why don't we try an apartment so we're not tied down. That way we can travel, sometimes south and sometimes to visit the children, as the mood strikes."

Use these communication and decision-making techniques to revitalize your marriage, to bring you closer together as you enjoy this new stage of life. Use the techniques, too, to enhance all your human relationships. Whether you are married or not, other people are important to you. Other people, friends and family, become increasingly important as you move into the retirement years.

9

Friends

People need people. Unless you're a hermit, a dyed-in-the-wool people-hating isolationist, you probably feel incomplete without frequent contact with other people. Contact takes place in many ways, on many levels, from a "good morning" for the mailman to a heart-to-heart chat with a friend. But a lot of the free-and-easy give-and-take that makes up social interaction, a surprising amount of the human contact you probably take for granted, is tied to the routine of work. "I think I missed most going to an office," says a not-quite-adjusted-to-retirement accountant. "I missed knowing everyone, going to the cafeteria, having lunch—it's not all business, you know—talking Super Bowl, talking golf." This give-and-take, this comfortable interaction with other people, is interrupted by retirement.

The interruption may be a blessing in disguise, allowing you, at last, the luxury of personal choice. You won't have to go to that office, rain or shine, good mood or bad. And you won't have to play golf with clients or spend an evening with the sales force, not unless you want to. "Don't worry about needed friendships," a seventy-three-year-old retired school administrator comments. "Retirement offers the luxury of determining friendships by choice, instead of by expediency!" The interruption can also leave an unexpectedly large hole in your life, leaving you lonely and resentful—unless you take steps to build new friendships while maintaining old ones.

Friendships are always important, but they seem to become

more important as the years pass. There seems to be a definite relationship between the extent of social interaction and psychological well-being, a relationship that becomes more pronounced after the age of seventy. There may even be a relationship between social interaction and longevity. Loneliness, at least in the opinion of Dr. James J. Lynch of the University of Maryland School of Medicine, can lead to heart disease and premature death. This premise—that human interaction is essential to physical health—has not been proven to the satisfaction of the medical and scientific community. But few would question that, for most people, enforced isolation is unpleasant indeed. Few would question that, with age, people do tend to become more isolated—if they (we) allow it to happen.

Children grow up and away, involved in their own lives. Household responsibilities diminish. The job comes to an end, and so does the daily contact with others through the job. And friends, real friends, become all the more important. No matter how independent you may be, no matter how self-sufficient, friends—people who care—provide a framework, a mirror in which you can view yourself. Friends, even when neither you nor they put it into words, provide companionship and support, encouragement and approval, security and affection.

Friends are more than acquaintances, more than familiar faces to whom you nod hello when your paths cross. Real friendship involves more than casual chitchat about impersonal subjects, over the office water cooler or across the backyard fence. These encounters can be the beginning, but real friendship involves mutual sharing, and caring about each other. Real friendship takes time to develop. Real friends, kindred spirits, can find each other in an evening, but true friendship takes time to cement.

FOUNDATIONS OF FRIENDSHIP

Sometimes friendship is built on respect: "I've learned a lot from him" or "I really value her advice." Sometimes the respect goes the

other way: "It really builds my ego, the way he looks up to me."
Or as a humorist once said, we all need at least one friend who's
smarter, and one who's dumber. Sometimes friendship is based on
what sociologists call reciprocity, a willingness to help out: "We
don't get together often but I know if I ever need help—like when I
had the flu and couldn't get out—I can call Flo; she's the kind of
friend you can count on." Often friendship is based on compatibility, on a mutual sense of fun or a shared way of looking at
life: "We have a really good time every time we get together. We
hit it off the first time we met."

No matter how the friendship begins, no matter what you
most appreciate about your friend and your friend about you,
common interests and/or common experiences are essential.
Common interests are easy to define—and almost as easy to come
by: How many friendships are built on the tennis court or in the
bowling alley or in the bleachers? How many through a shared
interest in stamps or in sailing? How many friendships begin
because a couple like to play bridge and find another couple who
play at the same level and with the same degree of seriousness?
"We couldn't possibly spend an evening just talking with a lot of
our friends," says one woman, "it would be boring. But we're good
friends as long as we can play cards."

Experiences in common are something else. They are solely
related to time, to bridge games (or whatever) over the years.
"Friends you've grown up with—no matter how seldom you see
them—are always the best friends," says one Rhode Island retiree.
"We've lived in our town for twenty-two years, and have good
friends here. But we've spent our summers in the same town in
Maine since 1947. That's where our real roots are. Those are the
people who've known us longest, who've watched our children
grow up."

You may have little in common with an old high school
classmate other than the fact that you went to school together way
back when. But your memories in common may be enough to keep
the friendship alive. After all, who else would remember the wild

time you had the night of the high school prom? or the fire extinguisher fight in the hallway after the big game? Who else remembers you the way you were back then? Experiences in common, even when they don't go back quite so far, also cement on-the-job friendships. Have lunch day after day with a co-worker, gripe about the boss, share your children's triumphs, get to know each other fairly well over a period of years, and you would describe each other as friends. But when you don't see each other every day, when one of you retires, will you still be friends? "I still see the people I used to work with," one man says, "at least those who live in the same town." But what if you don't live in the same town? What then?

Look at your friendships. How many have been made on the job? How many are really friends? One measure: Are your friendships pigeonholed? Do on-the-job friendships stay on-the-job? Or have you developed other interests in common with co-workers? Do you play tennis with a colleague? go to ball games with another? entertain each other in your homes? Who does come to your house? Sidney Simon, whose values-clarification exercises are so useful in many areas, suggests that you actually make a list. Write down everyone you can think of who has come to your home to visit in the course of the last six months. Code the list according to whether each guest is a friend, a relative, or a business/community obligation. Code the friends according to the basis of the friendship: convenience? shared interests? compatibility? Which of these friends will still be friends once you retire?

"I'm a lawyer and most of my friends are lawyers," one man realized after making a list. "We get together with our wives, and inevitably the women talk about whatever they want to talk about (my wife is an artist, one of the others is a social worker, one a teacher), and we talk law. We either talk cases or we talk people. But law is all we talk. I can see where I may have a problem if I retire first."

Most work-related friendships do not survive retirement, not unless they have expanded beyond the work relationship. If lawyers only talk law, they will have nothing else to talk about. If they only talk law—or business, or shop—during the workday and not beyond it, there is no real friendship. "While I was there I was friendly," says a former assembly-line worker, "but I find that people that you work with, when the day is over, that's it. You go your way, and they go theirs." Friendships that don't last beyond the workday, it's safe to say, don't last beyond retirement. "No, nobody ever looked me up. But I say to myself, 'Well, how many people have *you* looked up that retired?' and I say, 'Well, it probably makes sense.' . . . I've been back once, and I don't have the urge to go back anymore. I have nothing in common with them."

PATTERNS OF FRIENDSHIP

You may have had mostly work-related friendships. You may have always had a great many friends, both on and off the job. You may have nurtured a few close friends, and seen no need for more. Long-lasting patterns, in friendship as in anything else, will continue to influence your behavior in the retirement years. If you've always been a loner, it won't make much difference to you if your circle narrows. If you've always had a lot of friends, it will make a big difference. "I'm a people person," says a retired salesman. "I've always liked a lot of people—and I miss the people from my job."

You may be happiest with many friends or with a selected few. You may like a wide range of people, or stick with those who are most like yourself. But be aware of the pattern you choose, and of its likely impact after retirement. Corporate lawyers who socialize with corporate lawyers, discussing corporate law and the person-alities they encounter, may not realize how narrow their interests are; the *retired* corporate lawyer, however, seeking to maintain a place in the circle of friends, may soon find himself out of touch. The person with broader interests, and a wider circle of friends, will not have this problem. "I'm fortunate in having friends in many walks of life—a stockbroker, a real estate man, someone in manufacturing," says a former pharmaceutical salesman, "so we never talked much business in our relaxing time. We get together and it's no different than it ever was. I forget I'm retired—unless it's a Sunday evening and we break up early because, as they say, 'It's a workday tomorrow.' "

You can stick with your old friendship pattern, or form a new one. The choice is yours. You can stick with old friends and true, strengthening the relationships which mean the most to you—and bearing in mind that time will, inevitably, take its toll. Or you can set out to deliberately expand your circle of friends, by making new ones. A combination may be best: making new friends while enjoying old ones. Or as an old Girl Scout song used to put it (and maybe still does): "Make new friends but keep the old/one is silver, the other gold." If you want new friends, however, you must be willing to reach out to other people. You have to consider, at least, dropping old prejudices. Must all your friends be the same age? Must they all be the same sex? Must they all, if you are married, be mutual friends, equally dear to both you and your spouse?

MAKING NEW FRIENDS

Most close friends are about the same age or, if not the same age, then roughly at the same stage in life. "Our babies were babies together; now we're looking forward to retirement together." There's something to be said for same-age friendships; shared experiences do build a common bond. But there's also something to be said for having friends of different ages; you can expand your own horizons by reaching out to people both older and younger. Most people realize this, at least in theory. "While the young may prefer to picture older people off by themselves," the 1974 Harris poll found, "spending a good deal of their time sleeping, sitting and doing nothing, or nostalgically dwelling upon their past, older people themselves are unwilling to be relegated to the sidelines of society. . . . Like the young, three out of four people 65 and over said they would prefer to spend most of their time with people of all different ages, rather than with people their own age only." Yet really close cross-age friendships, in practice, can be a pleasant surprise: "I asked my daughter's college friend to have lunch with me when she first moved to the city," says an older woman. "I thought at the time that it was just a friendly one-time gesture, since she knew few people here. But we discovered that we really like each other. We like the same things. We've become real friends. We confide in each other."

Cross-age friendship, like all friendships, takes cultivation. But the effort is worthwhile. "You'll retain a youthful outlook," says one man, a retired YMCA secretary. "And anyway, you can't make friends fast enough to replace those lost by age." If you're blessed with particularly long life, the loss of old friends can be a particularly poignant problem: one man, at one hundred and four, recalls his last friend dying when he was seventy-seven; he hasn't had a friend since. But even with a "normal" life-span, and many friends of similar age, younger friends offer a fresh perspective.

But cross-age friendships, like any friendships, cannot be forced; they can grow through mutual interests, any interest, as long as it is real. One woman, ten years retired from a job in advertising, has become great friends with a twenty-three-year-old. She began writing poetry after retirement, he began in college; they met in a writing group. They appreciate each other's poetry, enjoy long conversations filled with plays on words, and have become fierce competitors over Scrabble. With mutual interests, there is no generation gap. Poetry is a great leveler; so is square dancing; so is bird watching.

Most friends are not only the same age, they are the same sex; women confide in women and men spend time with men. It may be force of habit, it may be because interests differ, it may be because friends of the opposite sex seem to pose a threat to a marriage. In some instances, although far from all (and not as many as used to be the case), men and women do have different interests. Look at your typical evening out: Do the men discuss politics and sports on one side of the room, the women recipes and household problems on the other? Do the men discuss hobbies while the women tackle social issues? Look at your leisure-time pleasures: Do you go fishing or to a football game with male friends, leaving your wife to her own devices? Do you go antiquing with female friends, leaving your husband to whatever he wants to do? Or do you spend most of your time together? How would you feel about it if your husband had a female friend who liked football? Or if your wife took a male friend along on antiques expeditions? In most cases, sexual jealousy rears its head, effectively preventing such friendships.

Yet couple friendships, the basis of American middle-class married friendships, are the hardest to sustain. Look at the odds against all four people really liking each other. How many times do you put up with a couple because your husband likes them? or, at least, one of them? How many times do you go along because this is your wife's friend? When you are working, there is some room for individual friendships; you can always meet for lunch, although, even here, when the friend is of the opposite sex, you may hesitate. But what happens after retirement? Will you give up your individual friends? Even same-sex friendships can be hard to keep up, if your spouse is indifferent. But what will you do? Retreat into a cocoon of marital togetherness? It would be better not to.

Keep your couple friends, by all means. Become better friends with your spouse, too. But maintain and develop individual friendships as well. Otherwise, if you put all your emotional eggs into one basket, the eggs are all too likely to be shattered. For women, especially, the statistical odds indicate early widowhood: 80% of the men over the age of 65 are married, 40% of the women; 14% of the men over the age of 65 are widowed, 53% of the women. Put another way: there are 144 women for every 100 men over the age of 65. Women owe it to themselves, says Harold

Feldman of Cornell University, to develop close women friends over the years. "Stop seeing yourself in terms of the man in your life," Dr. Feldman urges. "Friendships with women are valid friendships, important friendships." And men, whose work-life friendships have often stemmed from the job or from social efforts made by their wives, also need friends of their own.

WIDOWHOOD

It's impossible to talk about aging and the retirement years, in view of the above statistics, without talking about the likelihood of being widowed. You probably don't want to think about it, but you should. You may die together, of course, in what insurance agents call a "common accident," but the odds are far greater that one of you will outlive the other. Widowhood is devastating, for men no less than for women, although women—because they are more likely to be widowed and because so many older women are both financially and emotionally dependent—get most of the publicity. Widowhood is devastating, no matter how well prepared you may be, but preparation, both practical and emotional, can remove some of the sting.

On the practical front, talk to each other. Share with each other, if you haven't yet done so, all the information the survivor would need to keep going. One of you probably has shouldered most of the financial responsibility over the years. Whichever one that is should now share the details: How much insurance is there? Where are the policies? In what banks do you have deposits? Where are the bankbooks? the safe-deposit key? What other investments are there? Who is your insurance agent? stockbroker? accountant? lawyer? Are there debts outstanding? Is there a will? Where is it? Sit down together, when you retire if not before, and go over all the financial facts of life. Write down whatever is necessary, then file the information and forget it. Don't assume, by the way, that it's always husbands who must share this information with wives. "My husband has absolutely no interest in such things," one woman reports, on behalf of many. "I had to take him by the hand and show him where I keep the safe-deposit key."

One of you, similarly, has probably shouldered most of the household responsibility over the years. Whichever one that is should now share the details: How do the kitchen and laundry appliances operate? Who do you call on for necessary repairs? Where do you keep the vacuum cleaner? How do you shut off the household water supply or the gas line? How do you make a simple meal? One intelligent sixty-nine-year-old man, an insurance executive on the verge of retirement, was completely at a loss when his wife went into the hospital for two short days. After years of plugging in a coffeepot every morning, a coffeepot his wife made ready the night before, he couldn't figure out which percolator compartment got the coffee.

On the emotional front, the best preparation is: Be a person. You've got to plan for retirement, if you're married, as a couple. You will find yourselves becoming closer in retirement, more companionable, and more dependent on each other. But don't invest yourself so completely in the role of spouse that you have no other identity. Don't be so dependent on your spouse that you cannot function alone. Have your own interests, have your own friends, while having interests and friends in common. "Before my husband's death, I was absorbed in my family and nothing else," says one widow, "and I'm not sure that's always a good thing. . . . After he died, I would have built a wall around myself, but friends pushed me out and into activities. It would have been easier if I'd belonged to something before."

Widowhood is one of the most stressful events of life—but stress is eased by friends. One study reported that 61% of older women anticipated loneliness after their husbands died, but only 29% actually suffered prolonged loneliness. Those who had frequent contact with friends, and satisfying activities, adjusted to their new lives. Some, after the shock wears off, actually enjoy it. Doesn't widowhood change your life, one woman was asked. "It sure does," she replied. "It's wonderful to be completely independent. I can make my own decisions, and I'm proud that I can."

Few women, or men, are actually happy to be widowed. But it is a good feeling to know that you can be independent, that you can take care of yourself if you must, and that you have friends who care and who will lend emotional support when necessary. One of the most positive things you can do, as a couple, is to build a support group of friends. A close group of friends can cushion you against loss, the loss of your job or the loss of a spouse. A close group of friends takes the place of an extended family, and may even be closer than family. A support group can be informal, developed over the years through long association with people. Or it can be somewhat more formal, developed by couples who deliberately set out to form a support network: "We get together once a month, in different people's houses, to talk—or, as our younger members put it, to rap. We're all different ages, so we talk about finding jobs and problems with children and feelings about getting older. It really helps to get these things off your chest, with people who don't criticize but just listen." This kind of support network, advocated by Sidney Simon, should meet regularly; as the members get to understand each other through their day-to-day concerns, they become more able to lend support in times of crisis.

The willingness to listen, to offer support without criticism or judgment, can be lifesaving when a friend is widowed. If you have a friend who has been widowed, listen to remembrances; don't squelch them, urging your friend to look to the future. But don't be overly and endlessly solicitous either; for years, one widow remembers, people were being "kind"—when what she wanted was someone just willing to talk. Be a friend, in other words, valuing in your friend what you have always valued, and offering in friendship what you have always offered.

THE FINE ART OF BEING SINGLE

If you head toward the retirement years alone, whether because you are widowed early or divorced or never married, you know that you need and want friends. You probably already have an informal, if not a formal, support network. But you may want to take additional steps before you retire.

One woman, for instance, realizing that her only family consisted of two nephews and not wanting to be dependent on them, either emotionally or financially, investigated life-care housing while she was still active and energetic. "I'm not ready for this," she confided at the age of seventy-four (after being on a waiting list for many years and, finally, getting in), "but I must get in now, to make friends, so when I leave the residence part for the hospital part of the home I'll have nearby friends to visit me." At seventy-seven, she's getting used to "living with a lot of old people." She's still active and involved, going out into the community on a regular basis. And she's happy, knowing that she has good friends and a secure future.

Another woman, the manager of benefits for a large company, took a long hard look at her life when she turned fifty-eight. Never married and dedicated to her job, she lived in an efficiency apartment, frequently worked late, and had few friends or interests apart from work—although she was listed as a volunteer in a local hospital and as a member of a couple of clubs. In preparation for retirement she bought a house, bought one hundred rosebushes and five hundred bulbs, got a gardener to set up a garden for her, and asked for more responsibility at the hospital. In two years she had built her volunteer job up to a responsible position, by deliberately making time for it in addition to her on-the-job responsibilities. She became active in her clubs, too, instead of a paper member, becoming an officer and a necessary part of the organization. Through the hospital and the clubs, she met people, people who became good friends. This, says Phoebe Bailey of Action for Independent Maturity, is "a unique, disciplined, farsighted approach to retirement. She knew she needed friendship, a home, a reason for getting up in the morning. She set out to secure all three."

Everyone, married or single, needs friends. Some need many friends, some are content with a few. But everyone needs the kind of friend you can call up for a cup of coffee. Everyone needs the kind of friend you can call upon when you need a shoulder to cry on. Everyone needs at least one confidant, one intimate, one person with whom private thoughts can be shared, one person who can be counted on for emotional support. A confidant is someone with whom you can let your hair down, someone with whom you feel at home no matter what, someone you trust—and someone who trusts you.

But you can't have a confidant if you keep everything to yourself. How open are you? How willing to share your feelings? There's one way to find out, a way to see both how open you are willing to be and to see the people with whom you are willing to be open. Think of your life in concentric circles, with yourself at the center; progressively outward rings contain your closest friends or intimates, other friends, then people you know fairly well, and, last, acquaintances. Fill in the rings, mentally or on paper, with the names or initials of the people in your life. Then think about the kinds of things you would be willing to share with each group of people. The Super Bowl game, of course, could be discussed with just about anyone. But what about your relationship with your parents? If you're hurt by something they've done, or guilty about some action of your own, who would you tell? Who could you tell? What about your feelings about retirement? You might tell a casual friend that you were thinking about where to live, but would you tell that same casual friend that you're scared about retirement? Would you tell anyone? If you were faced with a serious problem, emotional or physical or financial, would you call on anyone for help? or battle it through alone? Who could you call on? What about your feelings if a friend were to call on you? Would you be annoyed at having to put yourself out? or flattered that your friend felt he could count on you?

Many people tend to be very private, to keep feelings bottled up, to avoid pinning a heart to a sleeve. And certainly you wouldn't want to constantly and indiscriminately share your feelings. But when the chips are down, when you need support, it's only friends, friends with whom some feelings have been shared, on whom you can count. It's important, therefore, to nurture friendships, to develop more in common with at least some people than a shared interest in bridge or bowling. It's important for women because they are so likely to be widowed. Three out of four women will outlive their husbands. And it's important for men, according to sociologist John Scanzoni, because "men are more likely than women to have depended entirely on their spouses to serve in the role of confidant." Women are more likely, in this view, to have kept in touch with family and to have had close women friends.

Look ahead. Picture the relationship that will mean the most to you in the years to come. Who is in your picture? Who will be important in your life next year? five years from now? ten years? Why are these people important to you? What can you do, in advance, to strengthen these relationships? What can you do to form new ones?

Pay special attention to keeping old friends. "How can you replace someone who's known you for years, who remembers you the way you remember yourself?" says one about-to-be-retired man. "I don't want to move and leave such old friends behind." Reach out to old friends, with your newfound leisure; share with them your new leisure interests, your thoughts and feelings. But skip the gripes. You'll have complaints, aches, and pains; so will your friends. They do not make for lively conversation.

But old friends move away, even if you stay put. "All our friends seem to be moving to Florida. We don't want to go," says one New Yorker, "but it's hard to start completely over." Old friends, inevitably, if all your friends are of similar age, will die. You can be left alone, indescribably lonely, if you fail to make new friends as the years go by. Emotional flexibility, the ability to reach out to new people, can make all the difference between pleasant years and bitter ones.

You can make new friends, if you set out to do so. You'll have to, if you move. So why not set out on the same sort of campaign even in your old hometown? Extend yourself a little. Be willing to take some risks. Seek people out. Talk to them. Start a conversation with someone at a lecture or concert or ball game. Join a club or group; go to a duplicate bridge center, take a course at the community college, volunteer your services in a hospital or day-care center, enroll in a Y or community center or club for seniors. Do whatever it takes to get in touch with people. Make your own group. One man met a friend at a diner twice a week for breakfast. The friend brought a friend, he brought another, until the "breakfast club" built to seven regulars. "We have a grand time," one says. "If the weather is good we may go for a drive after breakfast. Other days we just sit around and talk, tell jokes. It's a place to go, people to see, and it's fun."

Wherever you meet people, especially if you meet through a common interest, think of them as potential friends. And act that way. Be the first to reach out, to make an overture, extend an invitation. Be willing to make the first telephone call, and the second. Keep in touch. Don't stand on ceremony. What's the worst thing that can happen? If you've chosen unwisely, and the spark of friendship is not reciprocated, you may be refused. So what? More often than not, however, the people you reach out toward will be delighted. Most people are only too glad to expand their circles of friends, but are uncertain of how to do so. So reach out to the new acquaintances you're making through your expanded retirement activities, reach out to the people with whom you have lots in common. You'll be glad you did.

10

Generations

Family relationships, like friendships, become increasingly important with the years. As you shed the pressures of the job and the responsibilities associated with child rearing, you can relax and enjoy relationships with your family on new ground. Start to strengthen those relationships right now, preferably while you are still working. Make the time to do so. Otherwise you may find yourself abruptly cut off from the job and from human contact. "Work masks isolation," writes gerontologist Alex Comfort, "and in our work-dependent society the illusion collapses at retirement."

So start now. Get to know your children as adults if you have not already done so, make friends with your grandchildren, establish a new footing with your parents. Look ahead to retirement and the additional time it offers, and get to know other members of the family. Stop relying on your parents to keep you posted on family doings, and get in touch with your brothers and sisters, nephews and nieces, cousins, aunts and uncles. You will enjoy the feeling of family solidarity if you keep in touch—and you may even find that some (not all, that would be too much to ask) of these long-lost relatives become good friends.

Your primary attention, however, will be devoted to your children, your grandchildren, and your parents.

YOU AND YOUR CHILDREN

The average American woman is forty-five years old when her last child leaves home. Her husband is a couple of years older. The empty nest, then, the household without children, is something to which you have long since adjusted before you near retirement age. At this time, your children are probably long since married, and probably long since parents themselves. That process itself— your children growing up and becoming parents—altered your relationship in many ways. You are no longer responsible for them, financially or morally or physically. You are independent— and so are they. You can converse with each other as adults about adult topics. These things don't change because you retire. Retirement itself has no particular impact on family relations, but it may be an event that prompts you to reassess those relationships. When you retire, you will have more time to spend together and, in some ways, a new relationship to establish.

That relationship may be new, but it will, inevitably, contain echoes of the past. Did you let your children grow up and become independent? Were they willing to leave the nest? Is resentment left over from an earlier hurt? Can you and your children talk to each other without an emotional hangover? "Our son just doesn't want to grow up. Twenty-nine years old and he still comes to us for everything, for advice, for information, for suggestions. We would like to live our own lives, and we would like him to learn to live his as well." Sometimes, perhaps more often, the shoe is on the other foot: "Mother is still telling me to wear a sweater when she thinks it's cold out," says one exasperated thirty-two-year-old. "But I could laugh at that—if it weren't symptomatic of the way she offers advice on everything and constantly interferes with my life. She always has; it's nothing new. But she always makes me feel as if I'm still fourteen."

Much, of course, is in the eye of the beholder. The younger generation, according to the 1974 Harris survey, believes that parents give far more advice than parents believe they do. Forty-two percent of those under 65 claim that their parents or grandparents tell them how to run their homes; only 21% of the older generation say that they do. Subtle expectations, not necessarily expressed, may be the key: "My mother no longer tells me how she thinks I should run my home—but I'm very well aware of whether or not she would approve. I try hard not to tell my daughter—but she, too, knows how I feel about such things."

There may be a bigger conflict on the horizon. Traditional middle-class values support parental self-sacrifice for children, with the built-in quid pro quo that adult children will, in turn, help their parents should help be necessary. These values may be changing. In a 1976 survey, increasing numbers of young parents were found to be "self"-oriented, more interested in their own personal growth and well-being than in sacrificing for their children; in turn, this "new breed" of parents also believe that their children have no future obligation to them. You can see the conflict; you may even be in the middle of it. You, as a traditionalist, probably did sacrifice for your children (in attitude if not in fact), putting their welfare ahead of your own, with the expectation (implicit if not expressed) that your children would be available should you need them. Your children, however, may just be part of this new breed, bringing up their own children by a different set of values. What, then, are their attitudes toward you? How do those attitudes mesh with your expectations?

There are other potential scenes of conflict. If one child is favored over another, in childhood and in adulthood, the less-favored is resentful—and, surprisingly often, the favored is uncomfortable. If you take sides in marital disputes—whether you side with your child or, as happens, with his or her spouse—you can never win. If you take sides in a dispute between your children and their children, once again you've lost. "I'm not eager to visit my folks. I know they think I'm doing the wrong thing in making Jon get a job this summer. He convinced them that it would be 'educational' if he went to Europe instead. But we made our decision, and I'm not going to talk about it anymore."

Sometimes adult children are enlisted in the marital wars of their retired parents. That's another mistake. Depending on the kind of relationship you have with your spouse, as well as the kind you have with your children, you may be able to get away with: "*Please* tell Daddy to *do* something, to get out of the house; he's driving me crazy." Depending on the relationship, you may wind up with: "Tell your mother to leave me alone," in a tone of voice that means trouble. There is more than one elderly couple that communicates with each other only through their children, living together but not living together. That is no route to satisfactory retirement, or satisfactory anything.

Fortunately, although the emotional legacy of the past always colors the present, most retired adults and their adult children are linked by ties of affection. The sense of obligation may be diminished but it has definitely been replaced by a sense of affection. "We keep in touch because we want to, not because we must," says one member of the middle generation. "Now that I'm a parent myself, I appreciate my parents all the more and value their advice." You may have noticed such a development in your own children, and capitalized on it. You may, in fact, remember your own shifting relationships with your own parents. Young adults are very prickly about taking advice, sensitive about shedding the last vestiges of childhood and dependency. Later on, wiser themselves, they are more likely to welcome advice in the spirit in which it is given. At any age, of course, that spirit should be one of helpful guidance, not one of interference. We have to learn new roles as we march through life, and the role of parent must be replaced, at least to some extent, by the role of interested observer.

In any case, your children, with children of their own to raise and careers to make, are pressured by the same sort of demands that ruled you in earlier years. You may have increased leisure; they do not. They may welcome your visits. They are more likely to welcome them if they are short and sweet, and not excessively frequent. Again, perception rules the roost. How long is a short visit? How frequent is too frequent? Try to get out on the table, before you retire, what your expectations are about your retirement relationship. First, what is reasonable in terms of where your children live? If they are nearby, it's one thing. If they are far away, it's quite another.

Most older people, even though they do not live with their children (and never did; the extended American family, social historians are beginning to agree, is and always was a myth), do keep in close touch. Ninety percent, according to University of Chicago sociologist Ethel Shanas, live less than an hour's drive from their nearest child; between half and two-thirds live within ten minutes' distance. Dr. Shanas's findings were published in 1967 and, in the interim, American families have continued to be mobile. Nonetheless, in 1974, the Harris study for the National Council on the Aging reported that 55% of the people over 65 who have children saw those children within the last day or so; another 26% saw their children within the previous week.

Some adult children, of course, live far from their parents, across the country or even overseas. Contact can still be frequent, via telephone calls and letters, but there is of necessity less spontaneous interaction, less awareness of day-to-day events in the life of either generation. There are real questions: Should you call, or even write, when a medical test must be performed and the diagnosis is uncertain? Should letters be deliberately kept cheerful? and therefore sometimes superficial? How often can you manage a visit? How long can you stay without the visit turning from pleasure to duty? And how much, if one child lives far away and another nearby, can you lean on the latter without being "unfair"? Do you have a choice?

Now, bearing in mind the realities of the situation in terms of where everybody lives, what do you expect from your retirement relationship with your children? Do a planning-board exercise, Sidney Simon suggests. Write out your answers to the question

What do I want from the children, right now? Have your spouse do the same, separately. Think about it. What, to you, would be the measure of a good relationship? Given geographic possibilities, dinner together once a week? telephone calls every day? How about, wherever they are, remembrance of birthdays and anniversaries? How about sending the grandchildren for a visit? How about, perhaps, spending a vacation together? What, exactly, do you want from your children at this stage of your life? What can you realistically expect them to give?

It's a two-way street, of course; what do your children expect from you? Do they want and expect your assistance? Do they take it for granted, perhaps, that you will baby-sit, either on an occasional basis or regularly so that they can go out to work? Do they expect you to continue to be self-sacrificing, to help them financially? Do they, worse yet, expect you to conform to some image they have of expected behavior "at your age"?

Most adult children, of course, recognize that as they are independent so are you; as they resent interference in their lives, so do you. If such recognition does not exist, a heart-to-heart chat, with open communication on both sides, may clear the air. If they still fail to understand, well, it's unfortunate, but you owe it to yourself not to be constrained by the expectations of your children. As this book should have made clear, you are not automatically ready for the rocking chair just because you are retiring from work. You are not automatically elderly and frail and incompetent just because you are retiring from work. Quite the contrary. You are entering a new stage, one in which you are both fully able and entitled to live the life that pleases you.

That life may include a job, paid or volunteer, of which your children disapprove. "Why do you want to work in a hospital? That's so depressing. And it's not good enough for you. If you can't find a consultancy, you should just take life easy. You've earned it." Nonsense. The work in a hospital, if that's what you've chosen, may provide rewards, in a sense of being useful, that no consultancy, no lounging in the sun, could provide. If your children can't see that, tell them. Your life, if you are widowed or divorced, may also include dating and possibly remarriage. Your children may disapprove. They may disapprove because they are fearful that you are being exploited; they may disapprove because they are unable to see you in any role but that of parent; they may disapprove because they fear the loss of their own inheritance. Once again, assuming that you know what you are doing, the answer lies in communication. Try to talk things out with your children. Then, if they still disapprove, and if you are sure that you are not in fact being exploited, go ahead.

YOU AND YOUR GRANDCHILDREN

The reward for keeping on good terms with your children may be your grandchildren. There's much less worry and much more fun in this relationship, especially if you relax and enjoy it.

The "typical" grandparent, the sit-by-the-fire and tell-stories-about-the-past grandparent, hardly exists anymore; he or she has gone the way of the rocking-chair retiree. Most grandparents, whether or not they are anywhere near retirement age, are far too busy leading their own lives. But that doesn't negate the joys of grandparenthood. It just means that the style may be different. You may enjoy fun and games with your grandchildren, going to ball games together or carrying on a running battle in checkers; you may do this regularly, if you live nearby and if you have time on your hands, or you may do so only occasionally if you are busy with other things. You may stick to a more formal relationship, bringing gifts for the grandchildren when you come to visit the family as a whole. You may, if you visit infrequently, be seen as what Bernice Neugarten of the University of Chicago calls "a somewhat intermittent St. Nicholas."

You may have a style of your own. What your grandchildren most appreciate, however, may vary as they grow. Four- and five-year-olds, not surprisingly, appreciate indulgent grandparents; gift givers are welcome. Eight- and nine-year-olds, however, much prefer active fun-seeking grandparents, the kind of grandparents who are willing to sit down and play a game. Eleven- and twelve-year-olds, with the distance and self-centeredness of incipient adolescence, may be too busy with their own affairs to be much interested in a games-playing grandparent. "I've got to go to the ball game with my friends. I don't care if Grandpa comes to watch, but I can't wait to go with him." There are, of course, as vast individual differences among grandchildren as there are among grandparents—although it's safe to say that children of all ages love a grandparent who loves them, who takes the trouble to show personal interest. But if you are more comfortable with the gift-giving St. Nicholas role, you may find yourself closest to your grandchildren when they are very young and, again, although to a somewhat lesser extent, as they reach their teens.

Whatever your style, there are enormous rewards in being a grandparent. There's the reward that love generates love, that young children accept you and your love without criticism, and return it manyfold. There's the time you have now that you never had with your own children. "I can enjoy these kids. I never had enough time with my own." There's also the pleasure of enjoying children without the endless responsibility. "It's great having them visit," says one grandparent, "but it's just as great sending them home again." And there's the joy of sharing your experience, of sharing stories of the past and of the times when your grand-children's parents were young. Children "like to hear about the past," says Alex Comfort, "and telling them about the past has a function, so don't confuse this with doting reminiscence." If children don't hear about your past, in fact, they are missing a great deal; history lessons are no substitute for an eye-level view of events and they are certainly no substitute for a sense of one's own identity.

Here are a few ways to make the most of the grandparent-grandchild relationship. Try to visit, at least occasionally, without your children. If you live nearby, encourage the grandchildren to drop in; if you live at a distance, ask your children to send the grandchildren for a visit on their own. "I like to get to know my grandchildren," is the way one grandfather puts it. "That's not really possible when my children are here too and we're carrying on an adult conversation."

Try to visit with your grandchildren, at least occasionally, one at a time. In a one-to-one relationship you can get on a footing that's never possible in a group. "My son's middle child has always been so shy and quiet. It wasn't until we had Amy visit alone for a long weekend that we realized she really has a lot to say for herself. She's always been overshadowed by her sisters."

A little grandparental indulgence is just fine, but don't try to buy their friendship. Children, even when they appreciate gifts, are far more appreciative of your interest, and of time spent together. When you do give gifts, try to make them gifts, personally chosen, instead of money. If you must give money, give it directly. "My grandmother wants me to have something 'from her,' she says," a West Coast teen-ager complains, "but she gives my mother the money and tells her to pick it out. That's a cop-out."

Spend active time with your grandchildren, if at all possible. Share your interests and, in so doing, expand their world. Go hiking together, or camping; visit a museum, go to a concert; take in a ball game, or go bowling; work on your coin collection. Share *their* interests too, and expand your own world. You may even find that you like folk or rock music. Do things together, form a common bond, and you will be very special friends.

Enjoy the things you do with your grandchildren. Be proud of your relationship. Be at least as proud of your direct interaction, and of your grandchild's "self," as you are vicariously proud of your grandchildren's accomplishments. "My grandmother always tells me how wonderful I am because I get good grades, but I don't think she really knows me at all."

Lend an ear. Be available, if possible, when your grandchildren need support. But be tactful; don't repeat their confidences to their parents, or there will be no more confidences. And don't, even if you disagree with their parents, interfere. Your grandchildren won't like it—and neither will your children.

YOU AND YOUR PARENTS

"When I retired at sixty-five, I went back to my mother and father. . . ." Unusual? Not really. This former teacher is one of a growing number of four-generation families. As life-spans lengthen, more and more retirees have parents as well as children and grandchildren. As early as 1962, in fact, a three-nation study found that 40% of the elderly in the United States had great-grandchildren.

What does this mean for you, if you are approaching retirement as a member of a four-generation family? It can be very nice to have parents; it can also, depending on both physical circumstances and emotional expectations, be a burden. Example: A Florida man in his seventies, who hates to travel, must accompany his wife to North Carolina. Why? His wife's mother fell out of an apple tree. The "young folks," in their seventies, must care for her. Example: A mailman, looking forward to well-earned retirement leisure, finds that his mother has other ideas. Now that he is retired, she thinks, he has time to paint her house.

If an aging parent is ill, there is one set of problems. A sense of obligation, as well as affection, may compel you to alter your own plans to provide the necessary care. "There's no question about it. Mother needs help, and we have to be here to give it. But it's rough, no question about that either. We've always planned to travel once I retired, and now we can't." Even when an aging parent is reasonably well and independent, age inevitably brings changes; those changes may mean increasing dependence on you. It may take a long time: One sixty-three-year-old, planning his own retirement, hopes that he will be as energetic as his parents; in their eighties they roam the country in a trailer. Or it may happen sooner: The retired teacher who moved in with her parents found time for handweaving and for writing, at least at first. "Within a year, my father died, and my mother's health gave out. For the next six years I looked out for her and ran the house."

You're probably willing, if not downright eager, to provide the necessary support. But just as the emotional residue of the past affects your current relationships with your children, so the past creeps into your relationships with your parents. But now the position is reversed. *You* are the one who used to be dependent, the child looking to the parent for help and guidance. And your parent, formerly all-powerful, may now be dependent on you. The role reversal is hard to accept. "I couldn't believe it when I heard myself talking to my mother the way I talk to the kindergarteners I teach—'Now, let's eat lunch' or 'Why don't we go for a nice walk.' I was horrified." And the role reversal itself is accompanied by other, less conscious feelings. Are you still trying to prove yourself to your parents? still competing for their attention? still resentful over something that happened long ago? Are you still attempting to break loose and be your own person? Have you broken loose? Or do you still seek support and approval from your parents?

Your own personality will influence your relationship. And your parents' personalities will also influence the relationship. Don't expect them to change just because they are old. If your father has always been stubborn, he will continue to be stubborn; if your mother has always been anxious and fearful, she will continue to be anxious and fearful. You can't escape from a lifetime of behavior patterns, or from a lifetime of feelings. Resentments and conflicts and frustrations and dependencies of the early parent-child relationship continue to influence that relationship when the parent is elderly and the "child" is ready to retire from work.

Where adults are still dependent on their parents, the emotional devastation of parental aging is clear. Even where you are your own person, standing on your own independent feet, however, you will be markedly affected by your parents' aging. For one thing, of course, their visible aging makes you more conscious of your own slow but steady aging. It's possible to ignore the inexorable passage of time in ourselves—but not in our children, nor in our parents. For another thing, as long as you have parents, you have a layer of psychological protection. Whether or not you have much day-to-day contact, whether or not you ever seek advice or counsel, the very fact that your parents are alive is a form of protection. "It was awful when I realized, in the midst of mourning my father, that I am now completely alone. And not only am I alone, but I'm the parent generation, the protection against the world that my parents always were for me. I don't feel ready to assume that role. I don't even know if I can."

It's impossible to avoid all the practical problems and emotional conflicts associated with your parents growing old. But awareness of the potential problems, and advance discussion, can help.

Try to discuss with your parents, while they are healthy and independent, what should be done if and when they become ill and dependent. "Daddy and I have talked about it, and neither of us ever wants to go into a nursing home," one woman informed her adult children. "There's room in the house for someone to sleep in, and that's what we'd prefer." Such a solution may or may not be possible, even assuming financial capability, depending on the extent of the illness. But at least the air has been cleared by discussion, and the parents' preferences understood.

Don't anticipate problems, meanwhile, by seeing every memory lapse as senility, every ache as a forerunner of disaster; don't paint a mental picture of "old" and expect your parents to conform. Don't interfere with your parents' lives, any more than you want your children to interfere in yours. It's up to your parent where he wants to live, for example, and with whom. It's up to your parent, not you, to decide when to replace favorite possessions. It will be time enough for you to step in if and when your parent becomes unable to care for himself, unable to live safely alone. If forgotten pots boil over, if forgotten meals remain uneaten, you will know.

Meanwhile, when your parents do have problems, as they will, try not to take over. Don't encourage earlier-than-necessary dependency; it's to their advantage (and, of course, yours as well) if your parents remain independent as long as possible. Don't immediately assume that a widowed parent must move in with you; instead, encourage that parent to learn the skills necessary to live independently. Don't give advice about resolving a conflict, about where to live, for instance, or whether or not to join a group; give opinions, when asked, but not advice so strong that it must be taken. Then, whether your advice works or not, the responsibility, and the problem itself, becomes yours. And your parent is dependent. "Let the problem stay where it is," Dr. Robert C. Atchley counsels. "Let the person who has the problem solve it, but lend your support." If you "take over" the problem, if you internalize it so that it becomes yours, you are likely to become so tense that you provide less assistance in the long run. It's not easy to remain objective but it's worth a try, for your parents' sake as well as your own.

But do, at the same time, recognize the need for support. The elderly, especially as their friends and peers die and they stand alone, need your emotional support. They need it at the obvious times, such as the death of a spouse. And they need it at the less obvious times, such as the loss of a pet or the need to move from a long-cherished home or the need to give up driving. Loss in the later years is, unfortunately, both multiple and cumulative, and the loss of a pet, which may seem trivial to you, may be the last unbearable link in a chain of losses. The loss of a driver's license, even if relatively unused, may be symbolic of increasing isolation and dependence on others. Your assurances of transportation do not replace the symbolic loss. Try to see the real meaning of such losses, then, and don't point out to your parent how trivial the particular loss may be. Instead, provide emotional support by listening, by caring, and by just being there. That support can make a great deal of difference. It can make life more bearable and, some say, even lengthen it. Rejection, conversely, can cause depression, precipitate mental illness, and shorten life.

At the same time, a balance is necessary. Provide support for your parents, when it is needed, but find time to live your own life as well. It does no favor to your parents, or to the rest of your family, if you immerse yourself completely in their lives. You must also live for yourself.

Above all, do your best to communicate with your parents, using the same communication skills you use with your spouse: pay attention to what's actually being said, make yourself clear, express your feelings. It won't be particularly difficult while your parents are healthy and independent. As your parents become increasingly isolated with age and ill health, however, it will become more difficult. Try these two steps: First, let your parents reminisce, and listen to their tales of the past; your parents will feel better, and you may learn something. Second, try to interest them in the present by soliciting their advice, whenever you can. Don't shelter your mother from a grandchild's misbehavior, for instance, but ask her opinion about what to do; family members, of any age, are always drawn together by problems, and the most inward-turning octogenarian seems to snap back at the opportunity to feel needed and useful.

We all need to feel needed and useful. We all need to matter to each other. But, as always, we seldom tell each other what we really do mean to each other. You might sit down with your parent or parents and try the validation exercise you tried with your spouse. Take two minutes to share with your parents things you really appreciate about them, and ask them to do the same about you. Then use two minutes to tell them things about yourself you would like them to know and appreciate, and ask them to do the same about themselves. If your parents, trained in an earlier era to be modest and humble, find it difficult to say good things about themselves, you lead the way. Ask a series of questions: Who read to me when I was sick? Who never forgot a birthday? Who has always held the family together? Validation doesn't take much time and it's well worth doing.

Make the most of your relationship with your parents; it can never be replaced. And use this relationship as a guideline for your own future, in the practical arena as well as on the emotional front. On the practical side, look at what's happening with your aged parents and plan ahead for yourself. One sixty-eight-year-old, after facing the difficulties of finding a nursing home for his ninety-two-year-old mother-in-law, determined to locate a retirement community for himself, one with life-care facilities. "We're still active," he says, "but we won't be forever. People don't like to think about this, but we want to look ahead." On the emotional front, bolster your relationships with your own children, with other family members, and with friends. It should be clear, after dealing with elderly parents, that close human relationships mean more and more the older you get. The time to form those relationships is now.

Money

11
Money Traps

Money, the actual physical presence of dollars and cents, is undeniably important in retirement planning and in retirement itself. But attitudes toward money, how you feel about money and what it can and should do for you, are equally important.

Attitudes vary enormously, ranging along a spectrum from the realistic to the unrealistic, the objective to the emotional. It doesn't much matter how much money you currently earn or how much money you have in the bank. Attitudes have a life of their own. Two couples, the Y.'s and the T.'s, for instance, neighbors in an Ohio suburb, are in roughly the same bracket—not rich, not poor, but comfortably in between. Both had some rough times, when careers and children were equally young and belts were tight, but now that careers are established and children are grown, both are looking forward to a financially secure retirement. Both talk of travel, of taking life easy. But there are differences.

In the Y. family, there's never been too much discussion about money. Cash goes into a dresser drawer, to be used as necessary. Income over and above the cash needed for operating expenses goes into checking or savings accounts. The same amounts, more or less, are banked each month. But if Joan, a homemaker with an interest in art, sees a woodcut she likes, she buys it; if Sam, a commercial artist whose hobby is photography, wants a new piece of photo equipment, he goes right ahead and makes the purchase. They've talked about cutting back on such purchases as they approach retirement. Maybe they will, and maybe they won't, as they see how things go. But there's no disagreement, no argument, no frenzy.

The T.'s, on the other hand, have had many disagreements over money in their forty-one years of marriage, disagreements which almost fractured the marriage on more than one occasion. Jack, accusing Adele of extravagance, doled out money over the years, especially in the beginning, and insisted on an accounting of every penny, Adele, accusing Jack of miserliness, saved from her household allowance so that she could spend a little on herself. Their arguments over money, heated in the early years, finally subsided. Now, as Jack becomes nervous about impending retirement, tension is building again. And tension of any sort, in this family, erupts in a battle over money.

Attitudes toward money, whether you are married or single, can trip you up when it comes to managing your retirement finances. It's a good idea to take a look at those attitudes, to understand where you stand. As you approach retirement, after all, with its inevitable financial restrictions, you'll need all the clearheadedness you can get.

HOW DO YOU FEEL ABOUT MONEY?

How do you feel about money? Is it a source of stress? Frequently? or only occasionally? Do you become tense at tax time, once a year? At checkbook-balancing time, once a month? Do you forget about balancing the checkbook, and assume the bank is right, to avoid the aggravation? Does spending money in significant quantities make you nervous? What, to you, is a significant quantity? One woman, a nursery school teacher, has a personal limit. She will spend up to $45 for a dress without thinking about it. After $45 she not only thinks about it, she consults her husband. And he, as he repeatedly has told her, doesn't care.

This woman grew up in a family where her mother always consulted her father about spending. Her husband grew up in a family where his parents were each completely autonomous. Neither departed very much from the family pattern. Your parents' attitudes inevitably affect your attitudes—whether you follow their pattern or, rebelling, do the opposite. "My father was so awful with money," one woman recalls, "he made us all so miserable, that I vowed to enjoy the money I had. I'd much rather spend than save."

Many people would rather spend than save, whether or not they can actually afford to do so. In an affluent society, surrounded by the good things money can buy, it's difficult to resist. But depending on your emotional makeup and on your background, you may feel one way or another about that spending. You may feel guilty: "I know I shouldn't but I can't help myself. I get such a lift when I buy something." Or you may feel that it's your due: "I work hard enough, I can treat myself." However you feel about it, the actual habit of spending may pose a problem in retirement. If you are accustomed to buying what you want when you want it, putting the purchases on credit, you may want to think twice when the means to pay the bills is curtailed.

Do you have trouble viewing money objectively, as neither more nor less than a convenient medium of exchange? If so, you are not exactly alone. Money can and often does mean so much more: it may not buy happiness but it does symbolize status, power, love, and security, in different quantities for different people.

Money provides status, because it is a visible measure of accomplishment. But, and a big but: If all your status and all your prestige derive from the money you earn, what happens to you when you retire? What is your worth as a human being, independent of the money you earn? If your sense of self is inextricably linked to your income, you may be in trouble. If you view your prestige in the community in terms of your income, you may be in trouble. "Roger thinks that he's completely worthless now that he's retired. He just sits around all the time. There's enough money, but he feels less of a man because he's not earning. He thinks receiving a pension is a disgrace and he groans about it constantly."

Money represents power and control; the power of the purse needs no explanation. Parents control children with money, husbands control wives, employers control employees. Without money, people are powerless. You may remember early childhood feelings of helplessness. Did your parents control your behavior by doling out money only when they approved of what you did? Do they still manipulate you with the promise of an inheritance? Do you, in turn, use money to control others? Where does that leave you?

Money is often, too often, a symbol of love. It's undeniably easier for many people to show love with gifts than to express love with words, not necessarily good but easier. How do you feel about gifts? About receiving them from others? Are you pleased? or uncomfortable? What about buying gifts for others? And what will happen when your income is reduced? Will you feel less loved? less loving?

Money represents security, protection against whatever the fates may bring. This feeling is rooted in reality, especially if you have ever been poor. Jack T., whose insistence on penny-pinching has almost driven Adele to a divorce lawyer, grew up in a family where pinching pennies was essential to survival. He went into state civil service in the 1930s largely for the security it promised. But even with that security, he could never overcome his early conditioning. He came close for a while, after the children were grown and on their own, but approaching retirement, with the certainty of reduced income, threw him back forty years. He is terrified of the very possibility of insufficient income.

Money does represent security. True, of course, up to a point, but how much money makes you really secure? How much money cushions you against illness? How much retirement income will be enough? An "adequate" retirement income, like an adequate pre-retirement income, is subject not only to a financial yardstick but to your own perception. You may think you're in financial hot water and actually be in over your head; you may, like Jack, think you're in trouble and not be at all.

Look at your own needs, both practical and emotional. If your life-style demands more money, you will need more money. If prestige rides on visible wealth, you will want more money. If your emotional state requires a large financial security blanket, then you will not feel comfortable with less. If a reduction in income makes you worry, even if what's still coming in is compatible with your spending patterns, you will worry. If a cessation of earned income makes you nervous, even if you have more than enough stashed away to last your lifetime and more, you will be nervous. Budgets and statistical data and financial projections have nothing to do with it. You can and you should figure out your retirement finances, but do so recognizing that "enough" is not altogether a rational concept. How much you need depends, to a very large extent, on how much you think you need. Two people, can, in theory, have identical needs and identical income to meet those needs. One will feel secure, the other will be anxious.

People have different feelings about money. And people have different approaches to money management, personality-related methods of coping with the complexities of finance. How do you handle money? Have you always been prudent, keeping track of expenditures and squirreling money away for the rainy future? If so, you are demonstrating self-reliance—but you may panic at the thought of retirement. Or are you casually philosophical about money, not worrying too much because "I've always managed"? If so, psychologists would say, you are more secure. With faith in the way the world has always treated you, you don't see much need to worry—but you may be refusing to face facts. Either trait, of course, can be taken to an extreme. Prudence can become a compulsion to save, an unreasoning fear of the future. A happy-go-lucky approach can lead to unwise spending, to the accumulation of bills, that, once income is reduced, cannot easily be paid.

Look at your own pattern: Do you invest? or speculate? Do

you opt for the conservative, in whatever you do? or get a kick out of taking a risk? Do you keep a meticulous budget? or play it by ear? Whatever your pattern, it was formed by a combination of innate temperament and lifelong experience. It's too late to change it very much, and you will carry it with you, in much the same form, into retirement. Understanding your particular pattern, however, should help you to clear your way through the thicket of retirement finance.

You may be hacking through that thicket alone; or you may have company. If you are married, you each bring along your individual attitudes toward money, and the behavior based on those attitudes.

MONEY AND MARRIAGE

If you are married, you must come to terms not only with your own attitudes but with those of your spouse. You may have come to terms long ago, recognizing and accepting different ingrained attitudes toward money. "I've always been more willing to spend, Arthur to save. We balance each other." But that hard-won compromise may be tested anew if the prospect of retirement represents a strain to both your budget and your emotions. That strain may reactivate differences you thought long settled. "Arthur always said long-distance telephone calls were an extravagance, but I finally convinced him that it was the nicest way to keep in touch with the children, and a way we really could afford. But now that retirement is looming over his shoulder, he's going back to his old thinking, and yelling if I make a call. The phone bill gives him apoplexy. He can't believe that we won't die broke."

Sometimes the compromise is jeopardized by changing circumstances: Arthur has a justifiable if exaggerated concern. Sometimes the compromise is threatened by inability to adjust to new facts of life: financial security may have been attained but the habit of saving is too strong to break. "I'm a poor girl who will always be a poor girl," says a publisher, a woman in her fifties who has received a financial windfall but can't seem to spend it. "I can't change now." She is not alone, not in this generation. You probably have spent much of your life watching your pennies, first to survive the Depression of the 1930s, then to put your children through school, then for your own retirement. It's not easy to break the habit, even when the long-sought goal is at hand: the Depression is over, the children are grown, and your retirement is now.

If only one of you still has the saving habit, you may have a conflict on your hands. "My wife finds it more difficult than I do to get out of the habit of saving; she can't seem to realize how well off we are and how few years we have in which to enjoy our assets." If both of you still feel compelled to save, there may be no conflict but you may be depriving yourselves of a richly deserved retirement. Life may, of course, be longer than you think. And inflation will probably continue to exact its toll. But if you've assured an adequate retirement income, try to relax and enjoy it. Don't be the recluse, living close to the bone, who leaves cash and bankbooks for others to find. Don't be like the couple who saved for years, planning a post-retirement trip around the world, only to go into an emotional tailspin when it came to actually taking the trip: "We'd have to spend so much money . . . what if we need it later?"

Talk about money. When you sit down to plan your retirement budget (see Chapter 12), share your feelings about money. If you are married, you may say, your spouse should know where you stand and how you feel about money. But have you shared the information and the feelings? If you keep your salary and your investments a secret—"I give her enough to run the house. She doesn't have to know any more than that."—how can you expect your wife to adapt to a reduced budget? If you have never told your husband how nervous you are about the great unknown of retirement, how can you expect him to understand your feelings?

Have you communicated about money in the past? Who has always made the financial decisions in your family? Who has handled the books? Many couples start out thinking that they will handle everything jointly, discuss everything together, but such a system quickly becomes cumbersome and unwieldy. So the partner with the most financial expertise, or the most patience, takes over the paperwork, becomes the "family financial officer." Ideally, the other partner knows what is going on—but he or she may really not want to be bothered. Ideally, too, decisions—about major purchases, about whether to invest and where—should also be made by both parties. Sometimes decisions are made jointly; but sometimes they are made by the one who brings home the bacon.

If both partners earn money, decision making is more likely to be shared. But how do you regard that second income? Is it a help? or another source of conflict? Does it spark the arguments that revolve around money but aren't really about money at all? Do both salaries, in other words, go into the family kitty? Or is the "second" income considered extra money for the second wage earner alone? "My husband's earnings have always supported the household. Mine have been for me. Now that he's going to retire he wants to use some of my earnings for the household expenses, but I said nothing doing. We're not going to change the rules now." The rules, however, may have developed out of a different ball game: a young wife's part-time pin-money earnings, used for her own pleasure, are not really comparable to a salary earned in the retirement years.

Habits and attitudes—about the need to save, about the use of a second income, about the purpose of money—get all mixed up over the years. Even if you and your spouse come from similar backgrounds, even if you both stem from hardworking middle-class families, your approach to money may differ. Your values may be identical. But the behavior rooted in those values may be drastically different. An example: Two people, dedicated to sensible management of their funds, set out to buy new uphol-stered furniture for the living room. She says: "Let's buy the best we can afford. It will be well made and will last far longer than anything cheaper." He says: "Upholstered furniture is going to wear out sooner or later anyway, and it can cost almost as much to reupholster as to buy new. If we buy less expensive chairs in the first place we can just replace them when they wear out." Who's right? Who's being thrifty? And what happens when these same clashing views affect major pre-retirement purchases? The house, for example, needs a new roof. It makes sense to purchase the roof before retirement, while income is still coming in; both partners agree on this. But what kind of roof? with what kind of life-span? And what about coping with inflation, when even economists disagree? Is it wise to buy what you need, even taking loans to do so, before prices rise still further? Or is it prudent to put money away, to save at the highest possible rate of return, in an attempt to keep abreast with the diminishing value of the dollar?

These questions may be hard enough to resolve if you come from similar backgrounds. But what if you don't? What if your backgrounds were not the same at all? There are still class differences in so-called classless America. There are still class locations: the other side of the tracks, this side of the tracks, and the house on the hill. The very poor and the very rich, oddly enough, share a similar laissez-faire attitude, a willingness to spend. It's only the middle class, the vast middle class, that makes a virtue of saving. The very poor must spend what they have when they have it; on the other side of the tracks there is nothing extra to save. The very rich have surplus funds no matter what; the people in the house on the hill spend, by and large, as they please. The rest of us, those in the middle, always live with an eye to the future, putting money aside for what will happen and what may happen.

If you come from one place on the socioeconomic scale, with one set of values, and your spouse comes from another, with a very different set, you probably had early difficulties reconciling your approaches to spending and saving. Those difficulties, once settled, may resurface at retirement. The size of a savings account, that emblem of security, may be a source of paranoia to one partner, a matter of indifference to the other. As long as the account can be replenished, there is no problem; when the account begins to shrink instead, the problems—emotional at least as much as financial—may be catastrophic.

Sometimes, of course, attitudes and behavior don't differ at all. Sometimes both partners use money to meet their needs for status or control. Sometimes there's a mutual need to keep up with the Jones family down the block. Sometimes the need is for power within the family. Sometimes manipulative uses of money are occasional, the outgrowth of a rare power play in an otherwise rational couple: "We were saving for a trip to Europe next summer. But if Harold can buy himself an expensive camera, just like that, I can buy that new carpeting I've been wanting." Sometimes it's a permanent way of life, with results that can undermine a marriage—or, at the very least, disrupt retirement.

More than half the married couples (of all ages) who seek family counseling, according to the Family Service Association of America, report severe problems with money—but only 6% actually have inadequate income. The rest are in trouble because of unrealistic attitudes or because they use money, usually unconsciously, to meet emotional needs. The person who buys an expensive car may rationalize the purchase in terms of necessity— "that car has the power I need on the road"—but may, in fact, be acting out a need for status, for a sense of worth that can only be fulfilled through visibly expensive possessions. That may be okay if, and as long as, he can afford it. It may be disruptive if the money isn't there, if he is buying a Cadillac on a Pinto budget. These attitudes and expectations may work well enough in the income-producing years, in other words, especially if there is income to spare, but may need drastic adjustment to coexist with the reduced income of the retirement years.

MONEY AND FAMILY RELATIONSHIPS

Money rears its intrusive head into all aspects of life, including intergenerational relationships. As always, it's a handy way, or so it seems, to get attention and to exert control.

Gift giving is delightful, especially to grandchildren, if you can afford the gifts and if you give them with no strings attached. When it comes to spoiling your grandchildren, just slightly, you're entitled—up to a point. Try to be sensible, to strike a balance. If the yearning to continue to give gifts is indulged—"I've got to take lots of presents when we go to visit the grandchildren. I wouldn't feel right if I didn't"—it may wreak havoc with a retirement budget (and with how often, consequently, you see your grandchildren). If it is suppressed, it may wreak havoc with morale.

You may want to cut back, to substitute shared activities for fancy packages. Your grandchildren won't mind, once they get used to the idea. They really prefer your presence to your presents. If money is no object, you may want to break the habit anyway, for their sake as well as your own. You don't really want the youngsters to grow up to be materialistic, after all, and you don't really want them to see you only as Santa Claus. As for your children, they will probably be delighted. "I wish Mom wouldn't always bring such expensive presents for the kids," one young mother says. "It's not good for them. It makes it impossible for us, since we can't make them wait for anything. And, anyway, I would like the kids to look forward to her coming without automatically wondering what she's bringing for them."

If you find it hard to break the gift-giving habit, think about your motives. Are you, unconsciously of course, trying to buy attention or exert control? If so, you probably really know that it doesn't work. If your grandchildren scamper for their presents, and then scamper away, you're not getting the attention you want. Take another look at Chapter 10 for ideas on sharing yourself with your grandchildren, to get the quantity and quality of attention you deserve. If your grandchildren—or your children—seem annoyed and resentful, control is not worth the price.

When it comes to adult children and older parents (and you may, of course, be both, with a generation on either side), the promise of an inheritance can be the ultimate weapon, the ultimate form of control. Some people can joke about it: "Hey, that new carpeting is expensive. Don't fritter away my inheritance." But the inheritance can also become a threat, held over the heads of adult children to induce conformity with the wishes of the older generation. Choice of occupation, of residence, even of spouse, may be dictated by the person with the purse—if the other person, the potential recipient, goes along with the game. The threat may be spoken, or implied. And it may mask a very real hurt. "I've been buying my son and his family presents for years, but they don't even remember my birthday half the time. And Mother's Day? Forget it! Why should I remember them in my will?" You don't have to, of course, but will that make you feel better? Or would it be better to try to reopen communication, re-establish a relationship, now?

The threat may also lie in the other direction, if older adults deliberately deprive themselves of a comfortable standard of living in order to leave something to their children. It isn't necessary, or wise, to do so. It isn't always appreciated. "We supported mother for years," one fifty-six-year-old recalls somewhat resentfully, "because she gave us the impression that she didn't have any money. Then we found out that she did, but she had wanted to leave it to us in her will. We needed it more earlier, when our children were young. Now it doesn't matter."

The inheritance may be a joke. It may be a threat. Or most likely, it will not be discussed at all. Money, it has been rightly said, is the last great taboo subject: we can talk about anything and everything else, but we find it difficult to talk about money. Most often, between parents and children, money isn't even mentioned, although there may be hints here and there. The hints, too, may be ignored. "You're going to be around for years yet," adult child says to parent, thrusting aside any wish to discuss financial affairs. If your parents want you to know something about their affairs, accept the information; it will make them more comfortable. "You're going to get it all when I go," parent says to adult child. "You don't have to know how much it is." If your children are interested in your affairs, it may not be because they are grasping but because they want to know whether they can be of help—or whether they will need to help. You don't have to share the details, if you don't want to, but it might not hurt to fill them in on the broad picture. Think about it. Secrecy, at times, does more harm than good. Many people seem to think that it is not "nice" to talk about money and how important is is. But it is important. If you can talk about money, with those closest to you, it will be easier to plan for retirement.

Your income will be lower when you retire. It becomes more important than ever, therefore, to understand just what money means to you. It becomes more important than ever to sort out your priorities, to cut through the psychological underbrush that may stand between you and the retirement you deserve to enjoy.

If you've always taken things as they come, you probably will continue to do so. If you've always worried, you will continue worrying as well. Retirement won't change your basic nature. But the fact of retirement should make you stop and take a long hard look at your spending patterns. It should also make you look at your attitudes toward money. If money is and always has been a source of stress for you, retirement may throw you for a loop. But if you reduce that stress to manageable levels, you will be able to function. You can do that, you can assume control of your finances both practically and emotionally, by determining exactly what you will need and comparing it with what you will have, and then, if necessary, augmenting your income. The next chapter has the details.

Meanwhile, relax. Don't be excessively concerned about getting along in retirement. Most people find the anticipation far worse than the reality. But don't be excessively casual either. Money is important, and some planning is in order. A realistic appraisal of the facts, coupled with an understanding of how you use money, will help you to face the future with confidence.

12
Money Facts

When the psychological underbrush is cleared away, money still matters. This is not a handbook of technical financial advice. But practical money matters are, like it or not, a focal point of the retirement years. You will enjoy your retirement far more if you come to grips with your financial situation before you retire.

Most people simply don't know whether or not retirement will present financial difficulties. They, and probably you, think it will. But they don't know. Fully 40% of the people over fifty-five years of age, in one survey, could not estimate either how much money they would have in retirement or how much they would need. Many people tend to worry about money, about the reduction in income, as retirement draws near. Yet most people, according to study after study, find the anticipation worse than the reality. Sixty-two percent of the general public, in the 1974 Harris poll, believed that most people over 65 do not have enough money to live on; 15% of those over 65 found this lack of funds an actual personal problem. If 15% of the elderly are in financial straits, there is a real problem. But the fact remains, most people find that retirement is not the blow they expect it to be.

If retirement does not present financial difficulties it is because, for one thing, both Social Security and private pension benefits are at an all-time high. For another, you simply don't need as much to live on once you retire. "We can hardly believe how much more economically we can live now that we are both retired," a former secretary comments. "No daily expenses of getting to work, lunches, office contributions, wear and tear on clothes, use of car for business, et cetera, et cetera, all add up to a very considerable sum over the year." No wonder people over 65 feel so much more in control over their lives than people 55 to 64; they know where they stand, while the younger folk are only guessing.

It's time for you to stop guessing. It's time for you to be practical: try to determine, insofar as possible, how much income you will need in retirement; find out, in advance, how much you will actually have; practice, also in advance, living on that income; augment your post-retirement income if you can; and, not least, take care of all the financial odds and ends that will put your mind at rest.

HOW MUCH WILL YOU NEED?

The U.S. Department of Labor's Bureau of Labor Statistics publishes hypothetical annual budgets for a retired couple. According to the budgets for the fall of 1977, a lower-level budget for an urban retired couple, excluding personal income taxes, was $5,031. This is not intended as a poverty-level budget, the BLS is careful to point out; it's just a lower level of expenditure based on such variables as doing without air conditioning or taking advantage of free recreational opportunities. At the intermediate and higher levels, where belt-tightening is not as necessary, the average budgets rose to $7,198 and $10,711, respectively. These budget figures, along with inflation, rise each year.

It's comforting to have specific guidelines. But, as always, the actual dollar-and-cents amount you will have is not as important as whether it will meet *your* needs, *your* life-style, *your* psychological perception of security. For most people, however, retirement living does cost less. As the retired secretary commented, above, there are considerable savings inherent in retirement—unless, of course, you feel compelled to fill the empty hours with expensive forms of entertainment. If your tastes are quieter, two-thirds of your pre-retirement income should be adequate. To be on the comfortable side, with a margin for inflation, you might aim for three-quarters instead.

The only way to figure out just what you will need, however, is to take the tried-and-true if dull-and-boring way of finding out: sit down with pencil and paper (or electronic calculator if you're so inclined, but you should keep a visible record) and figure it out. Make a list of your operating expenses, as they are now and as you expect them to be after retirement: housing and household maintenance, food, clothing, transportation, medical and dental care, insurance premiums, taxes, entertainment, gifts, and personal spending. Some expenses, such as clothing and transportation, will probably go down when you are no longer working; federal income taxes and some local taxes also go down when you turn 65. Others, such as medical costs, may very well go up if you are no longer covered under your employer's health plan and if you require more medical care with advancing age. Then, after making your lists, see how much leeway you have. Some expenses are fixed (such as housing and utilities, if you stay in the same place); some are flexible (clothing and, up to a point, food); and some are optional (hobby items, travel).

If you plan to stay in the same place after retirement, it will be much easier to prepare your post-retirement budget; you know what it costs. If you plan to move, you may be in for some surprises, not only because moving itself is an expensive proposition but because living costs vary considerably from region to region, town to city. In addition to doing the pre-move research described in Chapter 7—scanning local newspaper ads will provide a lot of information about living costs—look at relative living costs on an overall basis, as calculated by the Bureau of Labor Statistics.

In the BLS statistics for retired couples, issued each summer for the preceding autumn, the index figure 100 is used to represent the average cost of an intermediate-level budget for all cities of the

United States. Cities over and under 50,000 in population, in four different regions, are then rated in relation to the index level. In general, it is less expensive to live in small towns than in big cities. In general, with the exception of the Washington, D.C., metropolitan area, it is considerably less expensive to live in the South than anywhere else in the country. In general, the Northeast is more expensive. But there are exceptions in every category: Bakersfield, California, has an overall rating of 93 while San Francisco is 111 and the Los Angeles-Long Beach area is 103. The Cincinnati region is 96, while Cleveland rates 104.

Within each area, furthermore, costs vary in different categories. The New York–Northeastern New Jersey region, with a relatively high index of 117, has a lower-than-average index of 75 in transportation. Where there are mass-transit facilities, and people do not need to own cars, transportation costs are lower. Some costs vary more than others. With the exception of Anchorage, Alaska, the most expensive city in the nation, most cities are higher in one category, lower in another. Baton Rouge, Louisiana, one of the lowest-cost cities, with an overall index of 90, rates 105 in the area of transportation and 51 (!) in terms of homeowner costs.

The moral of all this: It pays to investigate, and it pays to look carefully into things that matter to you. Will you plan, if you move, to own a home? or to rent? Will you plan to own a car? or want a city where you can rely on public transportation? The answers to such questions will affect your retirement budget calculations, and your retirement budget itself. Before you make too many decisions, however, take a good look at the income you actually will have.

FIND OUT WHAT YOU'LL HAVE

Much as you might like to move, to travel, or to plan any particular retirement way of life, a great deal will depend on how much money you can count on, as assets and as income.

Again, take out pencil and paper. Start by assessing your net worth. Make a list of all your assets: money on deposit in savings or checking accounts or Certificates of Deposit; stocks and bonds (current market value); U.S. Savings Bonds (current value); life insurance (cash value); annuities (surrender value); pension (vested interest); house (market value); other real estate, business interests and personal property. Against this list of assets, calculate any liabilities: the balance due on any mortgage or installment loan, taxes due, business debts, and so on. The excess of assets over liabilities is your current net worth.

Now look at those assets and liabilities, and estimate them as of the date of your retirement. Many of the assets may be larger: your house, given steadily escalating real estate values in most parts of the country, may be worth more; the cash value in your life insurance will have increased; your savings, if you have not withdrawn funds, will be earning more thanks to compound interest. If, of course, you foresee the need to draw on savings accounts or sell marketable securities, those assets will be reduced. At the same time, many liabilities may be either reduced or nonexistent. You may no longer, when retirement rolls around, be making monthly mortgage payments; your car may also be fully paid for; business debts may be wiped out.

Your assets are your financial cushion. Your income, both pre- and post-retirement, must now be measured against your ongoing operating expenses. Make a list of every kind of income, and then determine how much you will receive from that source now and how much you will receive after retirement. Include salaries, bonuses, commissions, tips, royalties, dividends, interest, rental property, Social Security, pension benefits, profit-sharing plans, annuities, and anything else that might apply. Match your expected income against your expected expenses. If the income is insufficient you may have to draw against your assets. Some of those assets, of course, are more available than others. The "liquid" assets—savings accounts and securities—also produce regular income. If you do have to draw against them, you will be reducing

Money Facts ·

that income and you must adjust your income figures accordingly. If you do have to draw against those assets try not to let the thought disturb you. Remember: You have been accruing those assets for just this purpose, to ensure a comfortable retirement. Just try to spread your withdrawals over a period of time, preferably a long period. You have an actuarially average chance of living to 78 if you are now a 65-year-old male; to be on the safe side, plan your retirement finances over a twenty-five-year period.

Before you think about reducing assets, however, be sure you know what your total income will be. If you, like so many others, run into a mental roadblock as you try to calculate your post-retirement income from pensions and Social Security, here is a must-do assignment: Find out, now, what you can expect to receive. You must find out in order to calculate your retirement budget. You must find out in order to have any peace of mind at all.

Social Security retirement benefits, which have risen steadily in recent years (especially since Congress pegged them to the cost of living), come in minimum amounts, maximum amounts, and average amounts; they come in the form of individual benefits and of spouse's benefits as well. A formula, based on what you've earned and for how long, will determine your specific benefits. Social Security, whatever you may have heard, is not an insurance system; your contributions over the years have not been put aside for your benefits. Social Security, instead, is a pay-as-you-go system with contributions by today's workers funding retirement benefits for today's retirees. Your benefits, nonetheless, are guaranteed by the federal government. But it is a complicated system, one in which it is very difficult for you, even if you know exactly what you have contributed over the years, to ascertain what you will receive.

To find out where you stand, ask your nearest Social Security office for a copy of the free leaflet "Estimating Your Social Security Retirement Check." It contains a step-by-step procedure for estimating the monthly benefit you will receive when you retire. Then, when you are within several months of retirement, visit your local Social Security office and, while you apply for your retirement benefits (they do not start automatically; bring with you proof of age, proof of earnings, and your Social Security number), confirm exactly what those benefits will be. Meanwhile, use the estimate for planning purposes.

If you are covered under a company pension, see the personnel office for details as to what you can expect. Don't wait until they get around to telling you. By that time you'll be so close to retirement that your planning will be seriously hampered. Details must be provided to you, by the way, in accordance with the Employment Retirement Income Security Act of 1974 (ERISA). Those details are extremely important in terms of the kinds of pre-retirement financial planning you will want to do. Find out:

- how the amount of pension benefit is calculated, and how much you can expect.

- how soon you are eligible for pension benefits and, if you retire earlier or later, how your pension will be affected.

- at what point those benefits become vested, so that you are entitled to them even if you stop working or change jobs.

- what options you have when it comes to protecting your dependents as well as yourself, and what you must do to elect those options. Under the 1974 ERISA legislation you will be assumed to have elected a joint and survivor option, under which your spouse continues to receive a benefit after your death, unless you reject this option in writing. With the joint and survivor option, your spouse's benefit is considerably smaller than yours, and your own, while you are still living, may be smaller as well. Find out just what your options are, and measure them against your needs, before you decide.

Both Social Security and private pensions are designed to provide a retirement income floor, usually as a percentage of pre-retirement income. That percentage varies with your income level. The new Social Security legislation, passed by Congress at the very end of 1977, provides that the average worker in years to come will receive 43% of pre-retirement income in Social Security retirement benefits; low-income workers will receive some 60%, and high-income workers proportionately less. Pension benefits are frequently pegged to Social Security to arrive at similarly staggered proportions of pre-retirement income.

Now that you have a complete picture of your post-retirement income, as complete a picture as you can possibly draw at this stage of your pre-retirement planning, you can begin to determine whether that amount will be adequate. One way to do this is to go beyond pencil and paper (at last!) and actually try to live on your projected retirement income.

PRACTICE LIVING ON YOUR RETIREMENT INCOME

Preliminary calculations about your retirement budget will come to life if you actually try to live on that budget. Miscalculations will become apparent, enabling you to correct them while you are still employed. Miscalculations may go in either direction: "I thought we'd need far more for entertainment than we actually do. I was thinking in terms of filling all that free time. But I wasn't thinking about the fact that all our friends are in the same reduced-income boat that we are. As a result, we play a lot of cards and do inexpensive things when we go out. So, we have a slight surplus, which is nice." Or on the other side of the coin: "I drastically underestimated what we'd need for transportation. We decided it would be cheaper not to own a car. But public transportation is not as conveniently scheduled as we had thought, we don't like to impose on friends, and cabs are expensive. We've had to take the money out of our recreation budget."

Some of these lessons, of course, can only be learned the hard way, after the fact. Living on your post-retirement income in pre-retirement days, however, can enable you to work many bugs out of your projected budget. But don't plunge in head first, and sharply curtail all your expenditures. One of the purposes of this exercise is to make the transition to retirement easier, not more difficult. One man, a former foundation executive, suggests the vacation approach: "Once you find out from the personnel office what your pension is going to be, take a vacation. On that vacation, you can begin to get used to the idea of retirement . . . and you can practice living on your retirement budget." Instead of going to a hotel, perhaps, rent a cottage, and implement your post-retirement food and recreation budget. You'll eat out sometimes, in retirement and on vacation, but you probably won't eat out every day; you may switch to lunchtime dining in restaurants, usually less expensive. You'll go to movies and shows, play golf or go bowling, but, again, not every day; you'll begin to take advantage of free entertainment and available discounts. If your retirement budget is on the lavish side, you may be able to indulge a passion for golf on this vacation; if not, bird walks and nature hikes and beachcombing, providing the same sort of outdoor exercise, may take up some of the slack. This is a good time to put your priorities under a microscope: Would you rather, if you must make a choice, eat out often or play golf? This is a good time, in fact, to put to the test some of the retirement activities you've been planning.

When you get back from this trial-run vacation, and when you are within a few years of retirement, start phasing down all your living expenses toward what your retirement budget will allow. You may never have kept a budget in earlier years, but if you're going to live comfortably on a reduced income, a budget of some sort becomes essential. Your lists of income and outgo are the first step in that direction. The second step is keeping track of all the miscellaneous expenditures you make without thinking about them—from candy bars and pipe tobacco to impulse purchases of personal clothing and garden equipment and workshop tools. When you keep track of these expenditures, and only when you do, you will begin to see what you can eliminate. You can refine your priorities: Would you rather, if you must make a choice, buy workshop equipment or build a vacation fund?

Then cut down on spending sprees. Pare down your optional

expenses, slowly but surely, until you reach a level that you think will be comfortable after retirement. Think in terms, perhaps, if you don't know what your precise retirement income will be, of two-thirds to three-fourths of your pre-retirement income and work toward that level. Do it gradually, cutting back slowly on optional purchases. If you do it gradually, it won't hurt; a drastic post-retirement change in life-style can hurt a great deal.

When you economize, both before and after retirement, do it sensibly. It doesn't save money to drive from store to store to pick up advertised specials. Any "cents-off" on the specials is more than offset in the cost of transportation. It doesn't save money to buy the large economy size that you'll never use. It doesn't save money to switch to cheaper brands that you don't like. And when you economize, always reserve some money for an occasional morale-boosting splurge.

Meanwhile, while you practice living on your retirement budget, you are still working and you are still earning money. Do two things: First, look to the future and make any essential major purchase (furnace, car, even a winter coat) before retirement, to keep capital expenditures to a minimum afterward. And second, invest any surplus; then you'll have more income-earning capital when you actually retire.

As part of your pre-retirement practice, too, start to adjust your financial cycle. You may be paid on a weekly or twice-monthly basis; your retirement income, you can be fairly sure, will be on a monthly basis. Social Security and pension checks, the foundation of your post-retirement income, will arrive monthly, and if your budgeting has been on any other basis, you are likely to find yourself in trouble. There's a psychological adjustment involved here as well as a practical one. "I always paid most bills monthly," a Montana man notes, "but I was paid weekly. I was used to thinking on a weekly basis—so much for food, so much for services like dry cleaning, so much for the checking account. I discovered myself doing all sorts of mental gymnastics when I went on a monthly basis. And until I got used to it, I found that there was never any money toward the end of the month. That's scary."

When you do your pre-retirement planning, try to convert all income and outgo figures to monthly terms. Look at your extra income from every source and try to arrange it on a regular monthly basis: Certificates of Deposit can be purchased from savings institutions, for instance, which provide monthly interest checks. Stocks can be purchased with an eye to the dividend months, so that you receive a check from one stock or another every single month. Try to get in the habit, too, of paying all your monthly bills as they come in. Bills left to multiply can destroy your retirement budget.

If, with all this careful planning in advance, your retirement needs exceed what you foresee as your retirement income, you will have to see what you can do, in advance, to build up that income.

AUGMENT YOUR POST-RETIREMENT INCOME

The first way to build your post-retirement income is by cutting down on your pre-retirement spending. If you reduce your outgo to what you expect to be able to manage later on, you should have a surplus from current income to invest toward that later date. Put another way, you can set a nest-egg goal and discipline yourself to build toward it before you retire. Either way, whether you save whatever you can or save specific amounts toward a specific target, surplus funds can add up to tidy sums.

If you have eight years to go until you retire, for instance, and want to build a nest egg of $25,000, you will have to save $2,500 a year at 6% interest; if you put the same amount into a Certificate of Deposit at 7½% interest, you will earn even more. That $25,000, if it continues to earn 5¼% after you retire (in an easy-in, easy-out savings account rather than in a higher-interest-paying but time-restricted Certificate of Deposit), will add $200 a month for fifteen years to your retirement income. If you invest in stocks and/or bonds, either directly or through a fund, you may secure still larger returns. But the chance of greater gain carries with it, inevitably, greater risk—risk you may not be able to afford if you must have guaranteed retirement income.

Before you decide on an investment vehicle, in any case, sit down and figure out how much extra income (over and above Social Security and pension) you will need; then figure out how much more you will want. Once you ensure your basic retirement through guaranteed investments, then, if you have surplus funds, you can take a chance to meet your "wants."

Using self-discipline to produce a surplus from current income, and saving that surplus, is one way, but not the only way, to extra funds. Another possibility is a second pre-retirement job—if you have the stamina and if it will be financially worthwhile. "I thought I was doing myself a favor by taking on private tax clients, and putting aside that income toward retirement," says a corporate accountant, "until I realized two things: it was costing me money to handle those clients, just to get to their offices, and the extra income was pushing me into a higher income-tax bracket. I decided to postpone doing that sort of work until after I retire; my tax bracket will be lower (Social Security benefits are not taxable), and I can earn up to several thousand dollars a year without reducing my Social Security check. It makes a lot more sense—once I convinced myself that I didn't have to earn more money right this minute."

Another way to produce income is to take advantage of property you own and only use part-time. Do you have a vacation cottage that sits idle most of the year? How much is it worth to you to have it available in case you decide to run up to the country for a weekend? Or would it make more sense to rent it out part of the year? A New Yorker with a summer cottage on the Connecticut shore of Long Island Sound, within commuting distance of several Connecticut colleges, decided to do just that. She rents the cottage to graduate students (they're more reliable, she feels, than undergraduates) during the school year and keeps it for family use all summer. Other people, with vacation homes in more isolated areas, rent out the home for part of the summer or part of the ski season, as the case may be. And others, who don't own vacation homes but do own a camping trailer or recreational vehicle, earn some extra spending money by renting out the equipment for part or all of a summer season.

Still another asset to evaluate before you retire is your life insurance. You've carried life insurance over the years to protect your family. Once your children are independent and your overall family obligations are reduced, you may not need as much insurance. Remember, though, that your pension (unless you have elected a joint and survivor option) will stop with your death. Your Social Security (although your spouse will receive survivor's benefits) will also stop. Keep enough life insurance to protect your spouse. But don't keep excess amounts. If you reduce your coverage or convert it to a paid-up form of protection, you may save substantial amounts in premiums. If you cash in the insurance, you can reinvest the cash value.

But don't drop any insurance policies without careful evaluation. Don't make any insurance decisions without consultation with a reputable and conscientious insurance agent, an agent who will inform you of all your options. And if you keep life insurance in force, be sure that the use of dividends, beneficiary designations, and settlement options are in line with your current wishes.

A careful evaluation of all your assets, and consultation with trusted financial advisers, should show you ways to increase those assets. Then there's one more step to ensure a comfortable retirement, comfortable both financially and emotionally: Wrap up all the financial odds and ends when you retire, and then forget about them.

A FINANCIAL GRAB BAG

The overriding principle to keep in mind, the only real way to wrap up all the financial odds and ends, is: get organized. Find out

what you have and where you have it, decide what you're planning
to do and do it.

Organize Your Papers. In the process of evaluating your assets and
setting up your retirement budget, you've shuffled a lot of papers.
Now is the time to organize those papers, to discard those you no
longer need and file those you do so that you can locate them
easily. Unless you're an accountant, or unusually methodical,
you're probably confused about (1) what to keep and for how long
and (2) where to keep what. "We had years worth of canceled
checks piled on a closet shelf, old tax returns in a bureau drawer,
receipts in a shoe box, birth certificates and Social Security cards
and my army-discharge papers in my desk. Insurance policies, car-
ownership papers and the deed to the house were all in the safe-
deposit box, along with some securities and E-bonds. We knew it
was a mess, but we didn't know where to start."

The place to start is with a simple rule: Anything irreplaceable,
or difficult and/or costly to replace—the deed to your house and
the ownership papers for your car, army discharge papers, securities, and E-bonds—should be kept in a safe-deposit box.
Anything which will be needed immediately in the case of death—
life insurance policies, Social Security cards, your will—should not
be in the box but kept readily available. Those things which are
kept at home should be kept together; a simple dime-store file box
will do, although a fireproof container is better. You won't be
overwhelmed with paper if you discard things regularly. Canceled
checks, for example, need only be retained for three years.
However, checks which might be needed to back up tax deductions should be kept for seven years. Records of investments—the
purchase price of securities, receipts for home improvements—
should be kept at least until you sell the property, longer if a tax
claim may have to be substantiated.

Make an inventory, so you'll know what you have and where
you have it. Keep a copy of the inventory at home, with a detailed
list of everything that's in your safe-deposit box. Keep a copy of

the inventory in the safe-deposit box, with a detailed record of all your possessions at home, including snapshots of artwork and other valuables. It's a good idea, in fact, to have a photographic inventory of your entire home; if you ever suffer a fire or burglary loss you'll have instant documentation to support your insurance claim.

Organize Your Estate. The only way to be sure that your assets will be distributed in accordance with your wishes is to make those wishes clear in a legally drawn will. Joint ownership of property is not a substitute. If you don't have a will, write one. If you do have a will, review it before you retire to be sure it is in line with your current wishes and with current estate-tax law. If you move, review your will with an attorney to be sure it conforms with state law. Some states require two witnesses, for example, and others three. Keep the signed original of your will with your lawyer or with your executor. Keep an unsigned copy at home, with a note saying where the original may be found.

Along with your will, prepare a letter of instructions to your family and/or to your lawyer or executor. This letter, which supplements the will, should provide the nuts-and-bolts information about your finances, list the location of all your important papers, and state your personal wishes. Include in your letter of instructions:

- a personal inventory, with description and location of all important items: Social Security cards, savings bankbooks (where is the account located? is it a joint account?), securities (where are they located? in whose name are they held?), real estate, safe-deposit box (where is the box? where is the key?), insurance policies, pension-plan documents, personal records (citizenship papers, marriage certificate, et cetera), tax records, credit cards, your will, jewelry, and other valuable property.
- a list of any debts owed, to you or by you, with complete information.

- a list of your professional advisers, with their addresses: attorney, accountant, stockbroker, insurance agent, banker, doctor.

- any personal instructions about your funeral, along with information about arrangements already made, plot already purchased.

Organize Your Credit Rating. If you've never used credit, never wanted it, establish a credit rating before you retire. It may be very handy to have and it may be very difficult to establish, once you no longer have a regular income. If you are a woman who has had credit in her husband's name, secure your own credit rating. "I always paid the bills. Jim never knew what was going on. But when he died I discovered I didn't exist as far as my charge accounts were concerned. They weren't 'my' accounts at all." The Equal Credit Opportunity Act of 1977 is supposed to rectify this long-standing inequity by establishing credit for both parties to an account. But it isn't automatic. You must apply. Don't take chances; establish your own credit identity, as an individual, and you won't be denied credit when you need it.

Organize Your Insurance. You've already reviewed your life insurance, as an asset. Now be sure that your beneficiary designation is in line with the beneficiary designation in your newly reviewed will. And review your other insurance needs. Your household insurance should keep pace with rapidly escalating property values; an escalator clause in homeowner's insurance can take care of this automatically, but check with your insurance agent. Your group health insurance may end along with your employment, and Medicare alone may not be sufficient; check into supplemental health insurance to bridge the gap. Convert your group policy if you can; it's probably the best buy. You have to apply for Medicare, by the way, and should do so before you turn sixty five; you are not enrolled unless and until you apply.

Organize your insurance policies, with a list for your heirs.

And be sure your insurance agent knows where you are. If you move after you retire, or if you plan to travel for extended periods, keep him informed.

Organize Your Tax Picture. Don't expect Uncle Sam to forget you just because you retire; considerable portions of your post-retirement income may still be taxable. Social Security benefits are not subject to income tax, but some portions of pension benefits, depending on how much your employer contributed and how much you contributed, are taxable. So is income from another job, from investments, and so on. Consult your tax adviser. Consult him, too, about the payment of your income taxes. If you have been accustomed to letting withholding taxes take care of it all, you must realize that you're now on your own. If you will have taxable income, you must file an estimated return and make quarterly payments of the tax due. If most of your taxable income will come from a pension or an annuity, however, you can arrange for the tax to be withheld. File Form W-4P with the agency that issues your pension checks and you will receive Form W-2P at the end of the year, just like the W-2 you have received all these years on your wages. Details are available from the Internal Revenue Service.

Be sure to take advantage of the tax benefits available to the over 65. You are entitled to an additional exemption of $1,000 on your federal income tax. You may, depending on where you live, receive property-tax adjustments as well as additional exemptions on state and local income taxes. If you sell your home after you turn 55, the 1978 tax law allows you a one-time capital gains tax break of up to $100,000. Taxes, never simple, seem to become increasingly complicated for older people, simply because of all these special provisions. As a result, according to testimony before the Senate Special Committee on Aging, as many as half of the people over 65 overpay their income tax. Don't let this happen to you. Secure advice from the Internal Revenue Service and, if you can, from a reputable tax adviser.

Before you complete your financial planning for retirement,

do two things: share your plans with your spouse, and be sure your plans are made with both the short term and the long term in mind.

If you are married, an absolute essential in pre-retirement planning is sharing information with your spouse. Share with your partner both the process of organizing your financial affairs and the finished product. If your partner outlives you (and the odds are that one, most often but not always the wife, will outlive the other), he or she must know what to expect; he or she must know where things are and what "things" there are. As you draw up your list of assets, establish your retirement budget, and write your letter of instructions, share the information with your spouse. Now is not the time for one person to shelter the other; the end result is far too serious.

At the same time, be sure that you look ahead, all the way ahead. Retirement is not a single unchanging span of time, from the day you leave work until the day you die. It can be considered, in fact, in three stages: the active and mobile early years, which can last well into the seventies, and for some people much longer; the slowdown period, in which you're still reasonably healthy and active but, feeling the impact of age, perhaps less energetic than you once were, less ready to tackle the world; and the last period, when chronic illness or disability may deprive you of independence. In making your financial plans, consider all three stages. Allocate your resources, if at all possible, so that you can enjoy the active years and be secure in the years to come.

Conclusion

13

A Time for Decisions

These years before retirement are a time for decision, decision in two major areas: what you will do in retirement, and when you will retire. The second decision is easier once the first is made. If, after reading this book, you have a well-developed plan for your retirement years, you will also have a clearer idea about when you want to retire. If you've decided to move into a second career, or to travel extensively, you may want to retire earlier, while both enthusiasm and physical stamina are at a peak. If you are enthusiastic about your present job, and don't see much in retirement besides boredom masquerading as uninterrupted leisure, you may want to postpone retirement.

Don't try to decide without considerable thought. You aren't talking about killing time for a couple of years. You must think and plan in terms of a good fifteen years, very possibly twenty or more, after retirement at the "normal" age of sixty-five. You must be willing to make long-term commitments. A full quarter of your life may be at stake, even more if you retire earlier.

WHEN SHOULD YOU RETIRE?

Mandatory retirement policies, while still present in many industries, seem to be on their way out. The decision about when to retire, therefore, is more than likely to be in your hands. That doesn't necessarily make it an easier decision; it may lead you to keep on working indefinitely out of inertia or the fear of a change. If you think you might want to retire, however, analyze your personal situation and then make your decision.

The first component in your analysis is facts: What is your employer's retirement policy? How much leeway do you have within that policy? If you don't know, find out. Then, what happens if you retire early? How much smaller is your pension? your Social Security? Are your other sources of income adequate? Are they large enough to take up the gap? If not, and you want to retire early, you will have to set out deliberately to increase that income. If you still have heavy financial obligations, if you are supporting elderly parents or putting children through college, you may not be able to consider early retirement—except, perhaps, in terms of a second career. If the mortgage is not yet paid up, or there are other personal debts, you may have to be sure of an ongoing income.

The second component in your analysis must be your own feelings. You may be able to afford to retire early, but you may not be the least bit interested. You know yourself well enough, after reading this book, to know how much of your self-esteem, how much of your identity, comes from your job. Do you have other sources of self-worth? How important are your off-the-job activities, the activities you plan to intensify after retirement? If you don't much like your job, you may be more inclined to consider early retirement. You may, in fact, be downright eager to get off the hook. But if you don't have absorbing off-the-job interests, that may not be a particularly good idea. You could then be going from the frying pan of a not-too-interesting job into the fire of boredom. You might then become the caricature retiree who sits on the front porch, or in the park, surrounded by unread newspapers, waiting for something to happen, for someone to pass by.

Another component in your evaluation is your physical health, your own and not that of some mythical elderly soul. You may, if your health is poor, choose to retire so as not to tax it further. You may, on the other hand, in exactly the same circumstances, choose to continue at a job you enjoy even at some risk to your health; it isn't only cowboys who choose to "die with their boots on." You may, in good health, want to stay at the helm. Or you may want to retire early to enjoy that good health. The definition of "early" may, of course, differ. As one eighty-year-old woman put it: "I retired at age seventy-five because I wished to have freedom while still in good health to enjoy theater, music, museums, and travel."

What are your retirement goals? What picture of retirement have you developed after reading this book, what personal image of your own life ten or fifteen years from now? How will that image change if you change the time of retirement? Will your financial situation, your feelings, and your physical health be greatly altered? If so, what will be the impact? And how can you weigh one against the other? Your financial situation may improve, after all, while your physical condition may deteriorate. You may develop new interests and have less stamina, and less inclination, to pursue them.

MAKING YOUR DECISION

The decision-making process always includes both rational and irrational elements. On the rational level are all the facts you can muster, all the reasoned discussion you conduct with the people who are important to you, all the lists you make with neat columns of pros and cons, advantages and disadvantages. On the irrational level are your feelings, your not-to-be-denied insistent feelings that one or another decision is right for you no matter what the facts may indicate, no matter what other people may suggest. If you have such strong feelings, don't try too hard to fight them. If you don't, if you are truly ambivalent about the best course to follow, then pay close attention to the facts.

Make the facts manageable, in any case, by dealing with them in small easy-to-handle units—and by calling it quits when you've marshaled enough. The retire-or-not question can be overwhelming if you confront it as a whole—and the question can be endless if you never call a halt. Divide the question into units and face each element one by one. If where you will live or what you will do or companionship with others is the most important factor, let that factor rule.

Make your decision as wisely as you can. Then live with it, without regrets. Live with your plans for the future, without sacrificing the present to needless worry. No matter how much planning you do, circumstances will change. You can't foresee all your needs, feelings, and interests in the years to come. So make the best decision you possibly can, given the facts at hand and your own feelings, and be comfortable with the decision you reach.

Whatever you do, don't retire *from* a job without retiring *to* something else, especially if you retire early. There are just too many years ahead. And whatever you do, whether you intend to move or stay put, to travel or take a second job or volunteer, remember that your first retirement decisions are not necessarily your last. Look far ahead to the fifteen or twenty or twenty-five years you may well have in retirement. But stay flexible. As you have evaluated all the options open to you at the outset of retirement, try, as you go along, to keep all your options open.

Appendixes

Appendix A

Facts on Aging

Test your knowledge about aging with the following quiz, developed by Erdman Palmore, professor of medical sociology and senior fellow at the Center for the Study of Aging and Human Development, Duke University Medical Center. Each statement is either true or false:

T F 1. The majority of old people (past age 65) are senile (i.e., defective memory, disoriented, or demented).

T F 2. All five senses tend to decline in old age.

T F 3. Most old people have no interest in, or capacity for, sexual relations.

T F 4. Lung capacity tends to decline in old age.

T F 5. The majority of old people feel miserable most of the time.

T F 6. Physical strength tends to decline in old age.

T F 7. At least one-tenth of the aged are living in long-stay institutions (i.e., nursing homes, mental hospitals, homes for the aged, et cetera).

T F   8. Aged drivers have fewer accidents per person than drivers under age 65.

T F   9. Most older workers cannot work as effectively as younger workers.

T F 10. About 80% of the aged are healthy enough to carry out their normal activities.

T F 11. Most old people are set in their ways and unable to change.

T F 12. Old people usually take longer to learn something new.

T F 13. It is almost impossible for most old people to learn new things.

T F 14. The reaction time of most old people tends to be slower than reaction time of younger people.

T F 15. In general, most old people are pretty much alike.

T F 16. The majority of old people are seldom bored.

T F 17. The majority of old people are socially isolated and lonely.

T F 18. Older workers have fewer accidents than younger workers.

T F 19. Over 15% of the U.S. population are now age 65 or over.

T F 20. Most medical practitioners tend to give low priority to the aged.

T F 21. The majority of older people have incomes below the poverty level (as defined by the federal government).

T F 22. The majority of old people are working or would like to have some kind of work to do (including housework and volunteer work).

T F 23. Older people tend to become more religious as they age.

T F 24. The majority of old people are seldom irritated or angry.

T F 25. The health and socioeconomic status of older people (compared to younger people) in the year 2000 will probably be about the same as now.

(Reprinted by permission of the author.)

The answers: All the odd-numbered statements are false; all the even-numbered statements are true.

Appendix B

Where Can You Afford to Live?

Comparative Living Costs, on an Intermediate Budget, for a Retired Couple Age 65 or Over

Note. In this table, based on Bureau of Labor Statistics figures for Autumn 1977:

1. Average costs = 100.
2. Personal income taxes are not included.
3. Nonmetropolitan areas are places with population of 2,500 to 50,000.
4. Housing costs include shelter, house furnishings, and house operation. For homeowners: property taxes, insurance, utilities, and repair are included. For renters: utilities and insurance on household contents are included.
5. "Other family consumption" includes reading materials, recreation, and miscellaneous expenditures.

AREA	Total Budget	Total Consumption	Food	Renter Costs
Urban United States:	100	100	100	100
Metropolitan Areas	104	104	102	108
Nonmetropolitan Areas	88	88	95	77
Northeast:				
Boston, Mass.	119	119	109	133
Buffalo, N.Y.	110	110	104	112
Hartford, Conn.	111	111	108	124
Lancaster, Pa.	99	99	102	90
New York–Northeastern N.J.	117	117	115	127
Philadelphia, Pa.–N.J.	104	104	112	108
Pittsburgh, Pa.	101	101	105	90
Portland, Maine	106	106	109	108
Nonmetropolitan Areas	99	99	104	105
North Central:				
Cedar Rapids, Iowa	97	97	89	98
Champaign–Urbana, Ill.	103	103	97	119
Chicago, Ill.–Northwestern Ind.	99	99	102	107
Cincinnati, Ohio–Ky.–Ind.	96	96	101	80
Cleveland, Ohio	104	104	99	109
Dayton, Ohio	95	95	97	90
Detroit, Mich.	100	100	98	104
Green Bay, Wisc.	96	96	89	96
Indianapolis, Ind.	99	99	97	96
Kansas City, Mo.–Kans.	99	99	98	81
Milwaukee, Wisc.	102	102	94	109
Minneapolis-St. Paul, Minn.	100	100	98	108

Homeowner Costs	Transpor- tation	Clothing	Personal Care	Medical Care	Other Family Consump- tion
100	100	100	100	100	100
107	101	102	98	101	108
79	96	95	106	97	77
168	109	104	92	96	114
121	117	126	96	94	108
111	117	102	119	96	116
94	108	100	88	94	96
161	75	95	103	103	113
108	88	90	92	98	107
99	110	95	94	98	106
104	109	117	84	96	106
109	105	101	103	98	77
95	104	116	100	98	105
92	107	120	105	100	108
83	94	97	98	102	109
89	101	106	83	98	108
105	109	108	114	97	113
77	103	103	87	99	109
94	109	102	102	102	109
84	102	106	92	99	107
93	110	107	91	98	110
86	108	111	108	101	108
106	107	120	96	99	109
95	105	104	100	95	111

AREA	Total Budget	Total Consumption	Food	Renter Costs
North Central: (Cont'd)				
St. Louis, Mo.–Ill.	98	98	103	79
Wichita, Kans.	97	97	93	100
Nonmetropolitan Areas	90	90	95	89
South:				
Atlanta, Ga.	91	91	98	77
Austin, Tex.	93	93	88	91
Baltimore, Md.	98	98	98	102
Baton Rouge, La.	90	90	101	65
Dallas, Tex.	94	94	91	91
Durham, N.C.	95	95	93	80
Houston, Tex.	96	96	96	85
Nashville, Tenn.	94	94	93	88
Orlando, Fla.	93	93	90	96
Washington, D.C.–Md.–Va.	106	106	102	113
Nonmetropolitan Areas	85	85	93	61
West:				
Bakersfield, Calif.	93	93	92	86
Denver, Colo.	97	97	97	78
Los Angeles-Long Beach, Calif.	103	103	95	116
San Diego, Calif.	98	98	93	107
San Francisco-Oakland, Calif.	111	111	100	125
Seattle-Everett, Wash.	108	108	104	124
Honolulu	113	113	123	151
Nonmetropolitan Areas	89	89	92	84
Anchorage, Alaska	138	138	122	219

Homeowner Costs	Transpor- tation	Clothing	Personal Care	Medical Care	Other Family Consump- tion
84	112	100	86	96	102
82	108	107	97	98	107
85	94	106	111	95	78
57	100	103	96	100	109
78	106	103	88	101	104
72	107	102	100	100	105
51	105	101	99	97	106
76	112	92	98	105	103
88	103	97	93	103	103
79	107	97	98	105	99
76	105	112	86	99	105
72	106	97	83	99	109
104	112	91	110	104	113
69	96	86	101	97	75
75	111	82	90	108	97
79	105	122	97	98	102
100	117	96	95	109	103
97	110	94	89	106	99
122	121	106	116	109	107
105	109	111	108	102	110
73	124	97	113	103	112
78	93	102	117	99	78
151	128	139	179	125	99

Notes and Sources

Myths and Facts
1. Retirement Is . . .

3–4   The Cornell study, after numerous reports in scholarly journals, was published as a book: Gordon F. Streib and Clement J. Schneider, *Retirement in American Society: Impact and Process* (Ithaca, N.Y.: Cornell University Press, 1971).

Other studies have also documented the relationship between planning ahead and successful aging. For example: David Schonfield, "Future Commitments and Successful Aging," *Journal of Gerontology* 28, no. 2 (1973): 189–96.

4   The fact that retirement itself is not a source of stress has been documented in several studies, including:

Streib and Schneider, *Retirement in American Society. The Productive Retirement Years of Former Managers* (New York: The Conference Board, 1978).

Robert C. Atchley, *The Sociology of Retirement* (Cambridge, Mass.: Schenkman Publishing Co., 1976).

4   "Fantasies tend to be negative,": Personal conversation with Daniel J. Levinson, August 11, 1977.

5   "What I wish: *Retirement Living,* September 1977, p. 36.

5   Statistics about men over 65 in the work force are from Patricia

Lee Kasschau, "Retirement and the Social System," *Industrial Gerontology* 3, no. 1 (Winter 1976): 11–24.

6   Statistics on changing life-span are from "Length of Working Life for Men and Women, 1970," U.S. Department of Labor, Bureau of Labor Statistics, Special Labor Force Report 187 (1976).

7   "emotional support system,: Personal conversation with Dr. William F. Westlin, April 19, 1977.

8   "There are fewer plop, plop, fizz, fizz days,": *Cornell Alumni News,* May 1977, p. 3.

8   Work-life expectancy of women, from "Length of Working Life for Men and Women, 1970."

9   Proportion of women in the work force from A. J. Jaffe and Jeanne Clare Ridley, "The Extent of Lifetime Employment of Women in the U.S.," *Industrial Gerontology* 3, no. 1 (Winter, 1976): 25–36. In 1974, 54.6% of women aged 45–54 were employed, 47.4% of women aged 55–59, 33.4% of women aged 60–64, and 14.1% of women aged 65–69. Only a minority of women, according to Jaffe and Ridley (in a somewhat unorthodox view), move in and out of the labor force. Most women stay in or stay out throughout their lives.

9   That women are as work oriented as men and as likely to confront similar problems in adjusting to retirement has been observed by Gordon F. Streib in a personal conversation with the author, August 29, 1977, and reported in the following publications:

  Robert C. Atchley, "Selected Social and Psychological Differences Between Men and Women in Later Life," *Journal of Gerontology* 31, no. 2 (1976): 204–11.
  Lillian E. Troll, Joan Israel, and Kenneth Israel, eds., *Looking Ahead: A Woman's Guide to the Problems and Joys of Growing Older* (Englewood Cliffs, N.J.: Prentice-Hall, 1977).

9   Statistics about moving from Atchley, *The Sociology of Retirement,* pp. 100–102.

9   12% live with their children: Beth B. Hess, *Growing Old in America* (New Brunswick, N.J.: Transaction Inc., 1976).

10 The "young-old" are defined by Bernice L. Neugarten, "The

Future and the Young-Old," *The Gerontologist* 15. no. 1 (February 1975), Part II.

10 Many studies demonstrate that retirement is not detrimental to the health. Among them is a study of five hundred men and women in the Boston area, reported in Alan Sheldon, Peter J. M. McEwan, and Carol Pierson Ryser, *Retirement: Patterns and Predictions* (Rockville, Md.: National Institute of Mental Health, 1975). Most of the people studied reported themselves to be in very good health. Fully one-quarter indicated that their health had improved after retirement.

10 The numbers of elderly Americans are cited by Merrell M. Clark, "It's Not All Downhill!" *Social Policy* 7, no. 3 (November–December 1976): 48–49.

11 Individual differences among older people are discussed by J. Myron Johnson, "Is 65 + Old?" *Social Policy* 2, no. 3 (November–December 1976): 10.

11 "the exciting aspect of medical care: Robert N. Butler, M.D., *Why Survive? Being Old in America* (New York: Harper & Row, 1975), p. 174.

11 Intellectual ability among older adults has been documented by the National Institute of Mental Health in *Human Aging II,* U.S. Department of Health, Education, and Welfare 71-9037. Psychological flexibility has been documented in the same study, and reported by Butler, *Why Survive?*, p. 370.

12–13 The Harris survey and its reports of misconceptions about aging are published as *The Myth and Reality of Aging in America* (Washington, D.C.: The National Council on the Aging, 1975).

14 "The person in the honeymoon period: Atchley, *The Sociology of Retirement,* pp. 68–71.

Also recommended:

David Hackett Fisher, *Growing Old in America* (New York: Oxford University Press, 1977). A scholarly but entertaining look at growing old, and at attitudes toward aging, throughout American history.

Simone de Beauvoir, *The Coming of Age* (New York: G. P. Putnam's Sons, 1970, 1972). A classic, if over long, look at aging and the aged.

Know Yourself
2. Who Are You?

20   Many of these exercises in self-understanding are based on the work of Sidney B. Simon of the University of Massachusetts, described in an interview with the author on August 26, 1977. For additional exercises, and more insight into values clarification, see Sidney B. Simon, *Meeting Yourself Halfway* (Niles, Ill.: Argus Communications, 1974).

25   Age roles are described by Bernice L. Neugarten, Joan W. Moore, and John C. Lowe in "Age Norms, Age Constraints, and Adult Socialization," Bernice L. Neugarten, ed., *Middle Age and Aging* (Chicago: University of Chicago Press, 1968), p. 22.

25   "when an older person simply behaves: Ashley Montagu, "Don't Be Adultish!" *Psychology Today* 11, no. 3 (August 1977): 49.

25   Men and women tend to view themselves: Marjorie Fiske Lowenthal, Majda Thurnher, David Chiriboga and Associates, *Four Stages of Life* (San Francisco: Jossey-Bass, 1975).

26   Role changes and the sources of role satisfaction are discussed in· two major studies:
            Suzanne Reichard, Florence Livson, and Paul G. Petersen, *Aging and Personality* (New York: John Wiley & Sons, 1962). Henry S. Maas and Joseph A. Kuypers, *From Thirty to Seventy* (San Francisco: Jossey-Bass, 1974).

27   "Family-centered" and "community-centered" leisure styles are described in Robert J. Havighurst and Kenneth Feigenbaum, "Leisure and Life-Style" in Neugarten, ed., *Middle Age and Aging,* pp. 347–53.

28–29 The three types of leisure have been identified by John R. Kelly, "Work and Leisure: A Simplified Paradigm," *Journal of Leisure Research* 4, no. 1 (1972): 50–62.

31–32 Hans Selye has written extensively on stress. For a recent example, see Hans Selye, interviewed by Laurence Cherry, "On the Real Benefits of Eustress," *Psychology Today* 11, no. 10 (March 1978): 60–70.

32   "Retirement is retirement: Frances M. Stern, director, Institute

for Behavioral Awareness, interviewed by the author on November 11, 1977.

33-34 Patterns of adjustment are described in Reichard, Livson, and Petersen, *Aging and Personality.*

34 Continuity of personality is described in Maas and Kuypers, *From Thirty to Seventy.*

34 Personality traits may remain the same,: Dr. Levinson discussed adult development in the later years in a telephone interview with the author on August 11, 1977.

34-35 Developmental growth in adults has been reported in:
Daniel J. Levinson, "The Mid-Life Transition: A Period in Adult Psychosocial Development," *Psychiatry* 40 (May 1977): 99-112.
Daniel J. Levinson with Charlotte N. Darrow, Edward B. Klein, Maria H. Levinson, and Braxton McKee, *The Seasons of a Man's Life* (New York: Alfred A. Knopf, 1978).
Roger Gould, *Transformations: Growth and Change in Adult Life* (New York: Simon and Schuster, 1978).
Gail Sheehy, *Passages: Predictable Crises of Adult Life* (New York: E. P. Dutton & Co., 1974, 1976). A book for the general reader, based on the research studies of Dr. Gould and Dr. Levinson.

3. What Do You Want to Do?

37 Fantasy as a useful tool in pre-retirement planning is described by Robert C. Atchley, *The Sociology of Retirement* (Cambridge, Mass.: Schenkman Publishing Co., 1976), p. 67.

37-38 "Imagery" described by Frances M. Stern, in personal conversation with the author, November 11, 1977.

39 Personal goals,: Atchley, *The Sociology of Retirement,* pp. 114-15.

42-43 The exercises on these pages are based on the work of Sidney B. Simon, University of Massachusetts, outlined in personal conversation with the author, August 26, 1977.

45 The relationship of occupations to things, to symbols, and to people is defined by the U.S. Department of Labor, *Dictionary of*

Occupational Titles (Washington, D.C.: U.S. Government Printing Office, 1977).

45 "Innovators" and "conformists" are described by Zena Smith Blau, *Old Age in a Changing Society* (New York: New Viewpoints, Franklin Watts, 1973).

46–47 Sex-related differences in job satisfaction are discussed by Alan Sheldon, Peter J. M. McEwan, and Carol Pierson Ryser, *Retirement: Patterns and Predictions* (Rockville, Md.: National Institute of Mental Health, 1975), pp. 88–92.

48 Personality "types" and the way in which they adjust to retirement have been identified by Marjorie Fiske Lowenthal, "Some Potentialities of a Life-Cycle Approach to the Study of Retirement" in Frances M. Carp, ed., *Retirement* (New York: Behavioral Publications, 1972).

49 Fewer than 15%: Richard H. Williams and Claudine Wirths, *Lives through the Years* (New York: Atherton Press, 1965).

51 People need occupation: Alex Comfort, *A Good Age* (New York: Crown Publishers, 1976), p. 124.

52 "We need continuity: Personal conversation with Herman Gruber, American Medical Association, April 29, 1977.

52 People who have made plans for retirement no longer fear the "unknown," according to pre-retirement surveys taken by the Equitable Life Assurance Society of the United States, reported by sociologist Yolanda Wesely in personal conversation with the author, September 27, 1977.

53 good decision making,: Personal conversation with Robert C. Atchley, October 1, 1977.

Options in Time
4. The Option to Earn

58 Second thoughts about a post-retirement job are described in Alan H. Olmstead, *Threshold: The First Days of Retirement* (New York: Harper & Row, 1975), p. 49. An excellent personal account of the first six months of retirement.

60 Get all the information: Personal conversation with Robert C. Atchley, October 1, 1977.

60   The Seattle experience was reported in *The New York Times,* October 3, 1977.

61–62 Helpful assistance in planning a second career (or a first) may be found in:

Richard Nelson Bolles, *What Color Is Your Parachute?* (Berkeley, Calif.: Ten Speed Press, 1972).

Charles Guy Moore, *The Career Game* (New York: Ballantine Books, 1976).

62   These examples, and many others, are drawn from Mark H. Ingraham, *My Purpose Holds: Reactions and Experiences in Retirement of TIAA-CREF Annuitants* (New York: Teachers Insurance and Annuity Association–College Retirement Equities Fund, 1974).

66   Small Business Administration offices are located in cities across the United States. If there is no office in your city, write to the SBA, 1030 Fifteenth Street, NW, Washington, D.C. 20416, and ask for their listing of publications. Your local library may also have a selection of SBA pamphlets.

66   A useful book for anyone, male or female, wanting to start a business is Claudia Jessup and Genie Chipps, *The Woman's Guide to Starting a Business* (New York: Holt, Rinehart and Winston, 1976).

66–69 A great deal of useful information on the job campaign, including myths and facts about older workers, may be found in "Back to Work After Retirement" (Washington, D.C.: U.S. Department of Labor, 1971). Available from the U.S. Government Printing Office, Washington, D.C. 20402; Stock number 2900-0130.

69   The 1974 Harris survey: *The Myth and Reality of Aging in America* (Washington, D.C.: The National Council on the Aging, 1975), p. 31.

5. Options for Personal Growth

71   People with a sustaining interest avoid "loneliness, boredom, and frustration—the three evils commonly associated with growing older." Julietta K. Arthur, *Retire to Action* (Nashville: Abingdon Press, 1969), p. 37.

71–72 Substantial numbers of management-level retirees: *The Produc-*

tive Retirement Years of Former Managers (New York: The Conference Board, 1978), interpreted to the author by Walter Wikstrom, in personal conversation, September 27, 1977.

73   Twenty-eight percent: *The Myth and Reality of Aging in America,* pp. 95–96.

74–75   For information on the Peace Corps, VISTA, or RSVP, check your local telephone directory or write to ACTION, Washington, D.C. 20525. For information on SCORE, formerly under ACTION and now sponsored by the Small Business Administration, check your local telephone directory.

78–79   "volunteer's bill of rights": Arthur, *Retire to Action,* pp. 62–63.

79   The men surveyed: *The Productive Retirement Years of Former Managers.*

79–80   People who help others have been found to acquire an increased sense of power over their own lives, and an increased ability to resolve their own problems skillfully and objectively. Elinor Bowles, "Older Persons as Providers of Services: Three Federal Programs," *Social Policy* 7, no. 3 (November–December 1976): 81–88.

81   "Don't count on your stamp collection: Mark H. Ingraham, *My Purpose Holds: Reactions and Experiences in Retirement of TIAA-CREF Annuitants* (New York: Teachers Insurance and Annuity Association–College Retirement Equities Fund, 1974), p. 79.

81   The college administrator turned weaver is cited (along with many other examples of active and involved older people) in Elizabeth Yates, *Call It Zest* (Brattleboro, Vt.: The Stephen Greene Press, 1977), pp. 94–102.

82   The traveler turned painter wrote about her experiences in the *Cornell Alumni News,* July 1975, p. 19.

84–85   Taking courses,: Ronald Gross, *The Lifelong Learner* (New York: Simon and Schuster, 1977).

85   For information on short residential programs for adults, see Wilbur Cross, *The Weekend Education Source Book* (New York: Harper's Magazine Press, 1976).

86   Information about CLEP exams may be obtained from the College Level Examination Program, 888 Seventh Avenue, New York, N.Y. 10019. There are regional offices in Bethlehem, Pa.; Evanston, Ill.; Waltham, Mass.; Atlanta, Ga.;

Austin, Tex.; Palo Alto, Calif.; and Denver, Colo.

86   Info about GED may be obtained from your local superintendent of schools, or adult education supervisor, or from the Adult Education Association of the United States of America, 1225 19th Street, NW, Washington, D.C. 20036.

86–87   Information about external degree programs may be obtained from:

> Board for State Academic Awards, 340 Capitol Avenue, Hartford, Conn. 06115.
>
> Thomas A. Edison College, 1750 North Olden Avenue, Trenton, N.J. 08638.
>
> Regents External Degrees, 99 Washington Avenue, Albany, N.Y. 12210. The National University Extension Association is at Suite 360, One Dupont Circle, Washington, D.C. 20036.

87   People can learn all through life,: An interview with Paul B. Baltes, supplied by the Pennsylvania State University.

87   The older learner may actually be: Roger DeCrow, *New Learning for Older Americans* (Washington, D.C.: Adult Education Association of the U.S.A.), p. 12.

88   Staying active keeps you involved in life,: Bernard A. Stotsky, M.D., "Coping with Advancing Years," in Leo E. Brown and Effie O. Ellis, M.D., eds., *The Quality of Life: The Later Years,* American Medical Association (Acton, Mass.: Publishing Sciences Group, Inc., 1975), pp. 120–21.

89   The "power of positive daydreaming" was described by Frances M. Stern in an interview with the author on November 11, 1977.

Options in Space

6. To Move or Not to Move

95   "If we yield: Avis D. Carlson, *In the Fullness of Time: The Pleasures and Inconveniences of Growing Old* (Chicago: Henry Regnery, 1977), p. 73.

95   "I moved from the city: Mark H. Ingraham, *My Purpose Holds: Reactions and Experiences in Retirement of TIAA-CREF Annui-*

tants (New York: Teachers Insurance and Annuity Association–College Retirement Equities Fund, 1974), p. 26.

96   "Even though I had gone to Florida: Mark H. Ingraham, *Trees in the Forest* (New York: Teachers Insurance and Annuity Association–College Retirement Equities Fund, 1975), p. 67.

96   "Presently, the days shortened,: Ingraham, *My Purpose Holds,* p. 24.

98   This is the house: Alan H. Olmstead, *Threshold: The First Days of Retirement* (New York: Harper & Row, 1975), pp. 8–9.

99   A small university town where they had once lived: Leo H. Baldwin, housing consultant to the American Association of Retired Persons, suggests that most people prefer to settle in the community where they have spent the most successful years of their lives—which may or may not be the community in which the day of retirement occurs. Personal conversation with the author, December 14, 1977.

99–100 "We looked for level ground: Ingraham, *Trees in the Forest,* p. 78.

100   If you move, you can even gloss the past: Thomas Collins, *The Complete Guide to Retirement* (Englewood Cliffs, N.J.: Prentice-Hall, 1970).

102   visiting the local Sears,: Marie M. Sorenson, *Move Over, Mama* (Modesto, Calif.: Osmar Press, 1977). A delightful personal look at retirement; available from Osmar Press, P.O. Box 126, Modesto, Calif. 95353.

103   urban conveniences become more important: Susan Sherman, "Satisfaction with Retirement Housing," *Aging and Human Development* 3, no. 4 (1972): 339–66.

104   "Human relationships: Personal conversation with Leo H. Baldwin, December 14, 1977.

105–6 Decision making and communication were discussed in personal conversations with Frances M. Stern (November 11, 1977) and Sidney B. Simon (August 26, 1977).

108   "We had friends,: Ingraham, *Trees in the Forest,* p. 4.

108   It does take time: A look at moving after retirement and the factors that influenced the decision for one couple may be found in Jean and Robert Hersey, *Change in the Wind* (New York: Charles Scribner's Sons, 1972).

7. Where Do You Want to Live?

110   If you are interested in moving to a warmer climate, you'll find detailed information in Peter A. Dickinson, *Sunbelt Retirement* (New York: E. P. Dutton & Co., 1978).

111   Statistics about where older people live are from "Facts About Older Americans 1976," (Washington, D.C.: U.S. Department of Health, Education, and Welfare), Publication No. (OHD) 77-20006.

111   Preference for retirement living in the North was described in *The New York Times,* February 1, 1976.

112   Preference for an urban environment was expressed in *The New York Times,* November 13, 1977.

115–16   If you choose a private home,: Before making any purchase, read one of the good how-to-buy-a-house books on the market. For example:

    A. M. Watkins, *How to Judge a House* (New York: Hawthorn Books, 1972).

    A. M. Watkins, *How to Avoid the 10 Biggest Home-Buying Traps* (New York: Hawthorn Books, 1972).

117   Condominium ownership is complex; consult an attorney with experience in the field. And read:

    Dorothy Tymon, *The Condominium: A Guide For the Alert Buyer* (New York: Avon Books, 1976).

    "Questions About Condominiums: What to Ask Before You Buy," (Washington, D.C.: U.S. Government Printing Office, 1974), HUD-365-F (2).

118–19   Statistics on mobile homes were obtained from the Manufactured Housing Institute. Before you buy, read "Buying and Financing a Mobile Home" (Washington, D.C.: U.S. Government Printing Office, 1975), HUD-243-F (4).

119   "In a conventional house: John Deck, *Rancho Paradise* (New York: Harcourt Brace Jovanovich, 1972), p. 52. A look at life in a mobile-home park.

120–21   two friends: Mark H. Ingraham, *My Purpose Holds: Reactions and Experiences in Retirement of TIAA-CREF Annuitants* (New York: Teachers Insurance and Annuity Association–College Retirement Equities Fund, 1974), p. 33.

123   For a study of five retirement communities, see Katherine

McMillan Heintz, *Retirement Communities: For Adults Only* (New Brunswick, N.J.: The Center for Urban Policy Research–Rutgers, 1976).

123 (85% of retirement-village residents: Heintz, *Retirement Communities.*

123 only 23% of the people: *The Myth and Reality of Aging in America* (Washington, D.C.: The National Council on the Aging, 1975).

123 "Don't 'hole up': Ingraham, *My Purpose Holds,* p. 30.

123–24 Reactions to retirement communities: Gordon L. Bultena and Vivian Wood, "The American Retirement Community: Bane or Blessing?" *Journal of Gerontology,* 24 (1969): 209–17.

124 The "good buy" that homes in a retirement community represent is reported in Heintz, *Retirement Communities,* p. 50. It was also reported to the author in interviews with residents of adult communities in southern New Jersey, December 9, 1977.

125 "It's like a reform school,": Susan Sherman, "Satisfaction with Retirement Housing," *Aging and Human Development* 3, no. 4 (1972).

125 "That an aging population: Jerry Jacobs, *Fun City: An Ethnographic Study of a Retirement Community* (New York: Holt, Rinehart and Winston, 1974), p. 4.

125 "Sure, we're old,": "Sun City: Heaven or Graveyard?" *The Record,* Hackensack, N.J., August 19, 1977.

126 "The home itself is secondary;: Personal conversation with Terry Bickel, December 9, 1977.

126 "We're a summer camp: Bill Paul, "Not Enough to Do? Consider Retirement at an Activity Home," *The Wall Street Journal,* June 10, 1977.

Human Options
8. Two by Two

132 "many couples reach old age: Bernard A. Stotsky, M.D., "Coping with Advancing Years," in Leo E. Brown and Effie O. Ellis, M.D., eds., *Quality of Life: The Later Years,* American Medical Association (Acton, Mass.: Publishing Sciences Group, Inc., 1975), p. 125.

133   "A lot of women: Personal conversation with Phoebe Bailey, January 17, 1978.

133   Greater appreciation for each other in the later years is cited in: Nick Stinnett, Linda Mittelstel Carter, and James E. Montgomery, "Older Persons' Perceptions of Their Marriages," *Journal of Marriage and the Family* 34 (November 1972): 665.
       Clark Tibbitts, "Older Americans in the Family Context," *Aging* (April–May 1977): 7.

134   Marital-assessment exercise adapted from "AIM's Guide to Communication in Marriage" (Washington, D.C.: Action for Independent Maturity, 1977).

134   Analyzing your own responses,: More ways to analyze your marriage may be found in William J. Lederer and Don D. Jackson, M.D., *Mirages of Marriage* (New York: W. W. Norton & Co., 1968).

136   Validation exercise told to the author in personal conversation with Sidney B. Simon, August 26, 1977.

136   Most people—some 80%: "Facts About Older Americans 1976" (Washington, D.C.: U.S. Department of Health, Education, and Welfare), DHEW Publication No. (OHD) 77-20006. This leaflet, issued on a regular basis, contains statistics on the older population: life expectancy, residence patterns, health care, income, and so forth.

136   people with close family ties: Suzanne Reichard, Florine Livson, and Paul G. Petersen, *Aging and Personality* (New York: John Wiley & Sons, 1962).

137   satisfaction is highest, according to Harold Feldman: Personal conversation with the author, Ithaca, N.Y., July 13, 1977.

137   "This period, when children are no longer at home: Harold Feldman, "The New Generation: Today's Older Person," talk given at the Annual Meeting of the National Council on the Aging, Chicago, September 17, 1973.

137   Harold Feldman's research into the marital life cycle has also been reported in:
       "Development of the Husband-Wife Relationship: A Research Report" (unpublished, August 31, 1964).
       Boyd C. Rollins and Harold Feldman, "Marital Satisfac-

tion over the Family Life Cycle," *Journal of Marriage and the Family* 32, no. 1 (February 1970): 20–28.

137   For more information on sex in the later years, see:
Robert N. Butler, M.D., and Myrna I. Lewis, *Sex after Sixty* (New York: Harper & Row, 1976).
Peter A. Dickinson, *The Fires of Autumn* (New York: Drake Publishers, 1977).

138   "We didn't have a plan,": "What I Wish Someone Had Told Me about Retirement," *Retirement Living* (September 1976): 20.

139   "Unfortunately," says one retiree,: Mark H. Ingraham, *My Purpose Holds: Reactions and Experiences in Retirement of TIAA-CREF Annuitants* (New York: Teachers Insurance and Annuity Association–College Retirement Equities Fund, 1974), pp. 92–93.

140   "It's been the worst six months: Marie Sorenson, *Move Over, Mama* (Modesto, Calif.: Osmar Press, 1977), p. 60.

140   "For weeks now,": Sorenson, *Move Over, Mama,* pp. 35–36.

140–41 housework can become: Personal conversation with Gordon F. Streib, July 29, 1977.

143   The sex roles inculcated: Marjorie Fiske Lowenthal, Majda Thurnher, David Chiriboga and Associates, *Four Stages of Life* (San Francisco: Jossey-Bass, 1975).

144   understanding is often clouded: Feldman, "Development of the Husband-Wife Relationship."

146   "I-messages.": Thomas Gordon, *P.E.T.: Parent Effectiveness Training* (New York: Peter H. Wyden, Inc., 1970).

146   Marriage Enrichment (sometimes called Marriage Encounter) was brought to the United States in the 1960s by the Jesuits. It is now available in most parts of the country under Catholic, Episcopal, Jewish, or interdenominational auspices. For information on the underlying principles, see John Powell, *The Secret of Staying in Love* (Niles, Ill.: Argus Communications, 1974).

147–48 Decision-making techniques are described in Robert O. Blood, Jr., *Marriage* (New York: The Free Press, 1969).

9. Friends

150   "Don't worry about needed friendships,": Mark H. Ingraham,

My Purpose Holds: Reactions and Experiences in Retirement of TIAA-CREF Annuitants (New York: Teachers Insurance and Annuity Association–College Retirement Equities Fund, 1974), p.99.

151 The positive correlation between social interaction and psychological well-being is cited in Bernice L. Neugarten, Robert J. Havighurst, and Sheldon S. Tobin, "Personality and Patterns of Aging," in Bernice L. Neugarten, ed., *Middle Age and Aging* (Chicago: University of Chicago Press, 1968), pp. 173–77.

151 The relationship between social interaction and longevity is the basis of James J. Lynch, *The Broken Heart: The Medical Consequences of Loneliness* (New York: Basic Books, 1977).

152 Foundations of friendship are described in Marjorie Fiske Lowenthal, Majda Thurnher, David Chiriboga and Associates, *Four Stages of Life* (San Francisco: Jossey-Bass, 1975).

153 make a list.: Personal conversation with Sidney B. Simon, August 26, 1977. Also see Sidney B. Simon, *Meeting Yourself Halfway* (Niles, Ill.: Argus Communications, 1974).

154 "While I was there: Alan Sheldon, Peter J. M. McEwan and Carol Pierson Ryser, *Retirement: Patterns and Predictions* (Rockville, Md.: National Institute of Mental Health, 1975), pp. 55 and 82.

154 Personality-related friendship patterns are discussed in Thomas Tissue and Larry Wells, "Antecedent Lifestyles and Old Age," *Psychological Reports* 29 (1971): 1100.

156 "While the young may prefer: *The Myth and Reality of Aging in America* (Washington, D.C.: The National Council on the Aging, 1975), p. 71.

156 one man, at one hundred and four,: Richard H. Davis, ed., *Aging: Prospects and Issues* (Los Angeles: The Ethel Percy Andrus Gerontology Center, The University of Southern California Press, 1973, 1976), p. 48.

156 The poetry circle was described in *The Record,* Hackensack, N.J., January 18, 1978.

158 Statistics on older people are from "Facts about Older Americans 1976."

158 Women owe it to themselves,: Personal conversation with Harold Feldman, July 13, 1977.

159   Be a person.: Robert C. Atchley, personal conversation with the author, October 1, 1977.

159   The importance of maintaining individual identity within the companionship of marriage is stressed by:

Bernice Hunt and Morton Hunt, *Prime Time* (New York: Stein and Day, 1974).

Helena Znaniecki Lopata, *Widowhood in an American City* (Cambridge, Mass.: Schenckman Publishing Co., 1973), p. 247.

159–60 One study reported: Frequent contact with friends eases the pain of widowhood. Clark Tibbitts, "Older Americans in the Family Context," *Aging* (April–May 1977): 8.

160   Support groups are recommended by Sidney B. Simon; personal conversation with the author, August 26, 1977.

161–62 "a unique, disciplined,: Conversation with Phoebe Bailey, January 17, 1978.

162   The exercise on feelings of privacy is adapted from Sidney B. Simon, *Meeting Yourself Halfway* (Niles, Ill.: Argus Communications, 1974).

163   "men are more likely: Letha Scanzoni and John Scanzoni, *Men, Women, and Change* (New York: McGraw-Hill, 1976), p. 477.

10. Generations

165   "Work masks isolation,": Alex Comfort, *A Good Age* (New York: Crown Publishers, 1976), p. 173.

166   Retirement may prompt reassessment of family relationships. Gordon F. Streib, "Intergenerational Relations: Perspectives of the Two Generations on the Older Parent," *Journal of Marriage and the Family* 27 (November 1965).

166–67 The younger generation according to: *The Myth and Reality of Aging in America* (Washington, D.C.: The National Council on the Aging, 1975), p. 78.

167   In a 1976 survey: *The General Mills American Family Report 1976–77: Raising Children in a Changing Society* (Minneapolis, 1977).

168   Affectional ties between the generations are noted in Streib, "Intergenerational Relations."

169   Ninety percent live, according to: Ethel Shanas, "Family Help

Patterns and Social Class in Three Countries," in Bernice L. Neugarten, ed., *Middle Age and Aging* (Chicago: University of Chicago Press, 1968), pp. 296–305.

169 55% of the people: *The Myth and Reality of Aging in America,* p. 73.

169–70 planning-board exercise,: Personal conversation with Sidney B. Simon, August 26, 1977.

170 you owe it to yourself not to be constrained: Harold Feldman, "The New Generation: Today's Older Person," talk given at the Annual Meeting of the National Council on the Aging, Chicago, September 27, 1973, p. 4.

171 The reward for keeping on good terms: Clark Tibbitts, "Older Americans in the Family Context," *Aging* (April–May 1977): 9.

171 Types of grandparenting behavior, and the "somewhat intermittent St. Nicholas," are defined by Bernice L. Neugarten and Karol K. Weinstein, "The Changing American Grandparent," in Neugarten, ed., *Middle Age and Aging,* p. 284.

171–72 What your grandchildren most appreciate,: Boaz Kahana and Eva Kahana, "Grandparenthood from the Perspective of the Developing Grandchild," *Developmental Psychology* 3, no. 1 (1970): 98–105.

172 The rewards of grandparenthood are described in Neugarten and Weinstein, "The Changing American Grandparent," in Neugarten, ed., *Middle Age and Aging.*

172 Children "like to hear: Comfort, *A Good Age,* p. 173.

173 The giving of gifts, and of money, is discussed in Grace W. Weinstein, *Children & Money: A Guide For Parents* (New York: Charterhouse Books, 1975), p. 50.

174 don't, even if you disagree: Tibbitts, "Older Americans in the Family Context," p. 10.

174 As early as 1962,: Peter Townsend, "The Emergence of the Four-Generation Family in Industrial Society," in Neugarten, ed., *Middle Age and Aging,* p. 255.

174–75 "Within a year,: Mark H. Ingraham, *My Purpose Holds: Reactions and Experiences in Retirement of TIAA-CREF Annuitants* (New York: Teachers Insurance and Annuity Association–College Retirement Equities Fund, 1974), p. 97.

175 Example of role reversal based on Barbara Silversone and Helen

Kandel Hyman, *You and Your Aging Parent* (New York: Pantheon Books, 1976). This book is an excellent resource for dealing with the problems of aging parents. Also see: Jane Otten and Florence D. Shelley, *When Your Parents Grow Old* (New York: Funk & Wagnalls, 1976).

175   Consistency of personality is described in Bertha G. Simos, "Adult Children and Their Aging Parents," *Social Work* 18, no. 3 (1973): 78–85.

177   "Let the problem stay: Personal conversation with Robert C. Atchley, October 1, 1977.

177   Loss in the later years: Simos, "Adult Children and Their Aging Parents."

177   Rejection, conversely,: Leonard E. Egerman, "Attitudes of Adult Children toward Parents and Parents' Problems," *Geriatrics* (June 1966): 217.

178   try the validation exercise: Conversation with Sidney B. Simon, August 26, 1977.

Money

11. Money Traps

183   Attitudes vary enormously,: Conflicts about retirement may be expressed in money terms, even when money is not actually a problem. James A. Knight, M.D., "Retirement: Financial Planning and Family Dynamics" (Presented at the Annual Meeting, Interfaith Council For Family Financial Planning, Minneapolis, June 3, 1974). For more information on the psychology of money, see:

    James A. Knight, M.D., *For the Love of Money* (Philadelphia: J. B. Lippincott, 1968).

    Edmund Bergler, M.D., *Money and Emotional Conflicts* (New York: International Universities Press, 1959, 1970).

186–87 An "adequate" retirement income,: Gordon F. Streib and Clement J. Schneider, *Retirement in American Society: Impact and Process* (Ithaca, N.Y.: Cornell University Press, 1971). Also: Gordon F. Streib, "Two Views of Retirement: In the

Clinic and in the Community" (undated, probably 1976 or 1977).

189   "My wife finds it more difficult than I do: Mark H. Ingraham, *My Purpose Holds: Reactions and Experiences in Retirement of TIAA-CREF Annuitants* (New York: Teachers Insurance and Annuity Association–College Retirement Equities Fund, 1974), p. 93. Also see: Mark H. Ingraham, *Trees in the Forest* (New York: Teachers Insurance and Annuity Association–College Retirement Equities Fund, 1975). Both report a survey of hundreds of retired college faculty, librarians, administrators, and staff.

190   If both partners earn money,: "Family Decision Making and Economic Behavior" in Eleanor Bernert Sheldon, ed., *Family Economic Behavior: Problems and Prospects* (Philadelphia: J. B. Lippincott, 1973), pp. 29–61.

192   More than half: Norman M. Lobsenz and Clark W. Blackburn, *How to Stay Married* (New York: Family Service Assn. of America, 1968, 1969; Fawcett Crest Books, 1972). An interesting book, including a chapter entitled "The Hidden Meanings of Money."

195   Don't be excessively concerned: In a study of five hundred retirees in the Boston area, the National Institute of Mental Health found that apprehension about financial restrictions and about post-retirement income was clearly worse than the reality. The study is reported in Alan Sheldon, Peter J. M. McEwan, and Carol Pierson Ryser, *Retirement: Patterns and Predictions* (Rockville, Md.: National Institute of Mental Health, 1975).

12. Money Facts

196   Fully 40%: Gordon F. Streib and Clement J. Schneider, *Retirement in American Society: Impact and Process* (Ithaca, N.Y.: Cornell University Press, 1971).

196   Sixty-two percent: *The Myth and Reality of Aging in America* (Washington, D.C.: The National Council on the Aging, 1975).

197   "We can hardly believe: Mark H. Ingraham, *Trees in the Forest* (New York: Teachers Insurance and Annuity Association–College Retirement Equities Fund, 1975), p. 73.

197   No wonder people over 65: Mathew Greenwald and Harris T. Schrank, "Personal Control, Demands on Institutions, and Age," unpublished, August 18, 1975.

197   hypothetical annual budgets: U.S. Department of Labor, Bureau of Labor Statistics, USDL 78-698, August 13, 1978.

198–99 the index figure 100: U.S. Department of Labor, Bureau of Lat or Statistics, USDL 78-698, August 13, 1978. Budget figures and comparative living costs are prepared annually and are available (usually in late summer) from the Bureau of Labor Statistics, Washington, D.C. 20212, or from any of these regional offices:

> 1603 Federal Building, Boston, Mass. 02203
> 1515 Broadway, New York, N.Y. 10036
> P.O. Box 13309, Philadelphia, Pa. 19101
> 1371 Peachtree Street, NE, Atlanta, Ga. 30309
> 230 South Dearborn Street, Chicago, Ill. 60604
> 555 Griffin Square Building, Dallas, Tex. 75202
> 911 Walnut Street, Kansas City, Mo. 64106
> Box 36017, San Francisco, Calif. 94102

The comparative index for Autumn 1977 will be found in Appendix B.

202   Pension information may be found in U.S. Government publications:

> "Know Your Pension Plan," U.S. Department of Labor, Labor-Management Services Administration, 1974.
> "Often-Asked Questions About the Employee Retirement Security Act of 1974," U.S. Department of Labor, Labor-Management Services Administration, 1975.

204   For suggestions on budgeting, see "A Guide to Budgeting for the Retired Couple," U.S. Department of Agriculture, Home & Garden Bulletin No. 194, 1973.

205   two-thirds to three-fourths: In an interview with James H. Schulz, professor of welfare economics (made available by Brandeis University, August 1977), Dr. Schulz said, ". . . there seems to be a general agreement that if you have pension income or income from any source that represents between 65 and 75 percent of average pre-retirement earnings in the last years prior to retirement, then one can reasonably expect to maintain a

standard of living that will not change radically from the pre-retirement years."

206-7   For basic information about investing in the stock market, write to the New York Stock Exchange, Dept. 180, P.O. Box 252, New York, N.Y. 10005. Ask for the "Investor's Information Kit" ($2).

207   Under the Social Security legislation passed by Congress in December 1977, retirees between sixty-five and seventy-two may earn the following amounts without reduction of Social Security retirement benefits:

   1978—$4,000
   1979—4,500
   1980—5,000
   1981—5,500
   1982—6,000

Those over seventy-two may earn as much as they can or wish, without penalty; in 1982 that advantage will be extended to those over seventy. As before, once the ceiling is reached, one dollar in retirement benefits is withheld for every two dollars earned.

211   Information about Medicare is available from the nearest office of the Social Security Administration. Ask for "Your Medicare Handbook."

212   Information about taxes is available from American Association of Retired Persons, P.O. Box 2400, Long Beach, Calif. 90801:
   "Tax Facts" is a state-by-state rundown of income, property, sales, and estate taxes.
   "Your Retirement Income Tax Guide" is a line-by-line guide to federal income tax.

A checklist of permissible income-tax deductions will be found in "Protecting Older Americans Against Overpayment of Income Taxes," from the Special Committee on Aging, U.S. Senate (Washington, D.C.: U.S. Government Printing Office, 1976).